Farmhouse
COOKBOOK

by Clarice L. Moon

Ideals Publishing Corp.
Milwaukee, Wisconsin

Contents

ISBN 0-89542-609-9

COPYRIGHT © MCMLXXVIII BY IDEALS PUBLISHING CORPORATION
MILWAUKEE, WISCONSIN 53226
ALL RIGHTS RESERVED. PRINTED AND BOUND IN U.S.A.
PUBLISHED SIMULTANEOUSLY IN CANADA

Caviar Rounds
Hot Tuna Canapés
Cornucopias
(page 4)

Appetizers and Beverages

ANCHOVY PECANS

Toast pecan halves in a 350° oven for 5 minutes. Spread bottoms with thin layer of anchovy paste. Press each 2 halves together. Serve immediately.

CAVIAR ROUNDS

Rye bread, toasted rounds
Caviar
Finely minced onion
Hard-boiled egg

Butter rounds of rye toast. Press on these rounds, slices of the egg white. Fill the inside of the egg white with caviar. Sprinkle finely minced onion over caviar. Surround egg white with grated yolk.

ASPARAGUS CANAPÉ

2 **T. mayonnaise**
2 **hard-boiled eggs**
   Pimiento strips
5 **asparagus tips**
   Toast triangles

Spread toast with mayonnaise. Chop egg yolks and whites separately. Arrange the chopped egg white and the chopped egg yolk in alternate rows across toast. Lay asparagus tips on top. Garnish with pimiento strips.

HOT TUNA CANAPÉS

Mix flaked tuna with mayonnaise or salad dressing. Add chopped stuffed olives. Add a few drops of Worcestershire sauce. Spread on toast strips and sprinkle with American cheese. Place under broiler until cheese melts. Serve hot.

CORNUCOPIAS

2 **3-oz. pkgs. cream cheese**
1 **T. pickle relish**
1 **T. minced onion**
12 **thin slices boiled ham**

Mash cheese with onion and drained pickle relish. Spread on a slice of boiled ham. Roll cornucopia fashion. Chill.

CHEESE SAVORY CANAPÉS

4 **T. Roquefort cheese**
2 **T. butter**
½ **t. salt**
⅛ **t. pepper**
   Mayonnaise
   Gherkins, thinly sliced
   Celery, minced
   Pimiento strips

Cream cheese and butter together. Add salt and pepper. Spread on toasted bread. Cover with celery mixed with a little mayonnaise. Garnish with sliced gherkins and a cross made of pimiento strips.

CHEESE BEEF STICKS

Cut American cheese in strips 2 inches long and ⅜ inch wide. Wrap each stick in a dried beef square. Place rolls on a cookie sheet, 3 inches below broiler. Broil until cheese is slightly melted.

EGGNOG

12 eggs, separated
1½ pt. cream or half and half
4 c. sugar
1½ c. whisky
1 t. nutmeg
1 t. salt
6 qts. milk

Beat egg yolks until lemon colored. Beat in sugar and salt. Slowly add whisky, cream, nutmeg and milk. Fold in well-beaten egg whites. Makes 2 gallons.

DIET SHAKE

1 12-oz. can diet soda, any flavor
⅓ c. instant nonfat dry milk
½ c. fresh fruit
⅛ t. artificial sweetener
½ t. vanilla
½ t. extract, strawberry, almond, rum or brandy
1 c. coarsely crushed ice

Combine all ingredients in blender. Whirl at high speed until frothy and blended.

SKINNY FRUIT WHIRL

1 12-oz. can diet creme soda
½ c. nonfat milk
1 t. lemon juice
⅛ t. artificial sweetener
⅛ t. salt
2 c. sliced nectarines, peaches or other fruit

Whirl all ingredients together in blender until smooth. Makes about 1 quart. Mixture may be frozen to make sherbet.

HOT TODDY

Juice of 1 lemon
2 T. honey or sugar
3 oz. bourbon or rye whisky
Boiling water

Put juice of 1 lemon in tall glass or mug. Sweeten with honey or sugar. Add whisky or rye. Fill glass with boiling water. Stir and drink.

RUSSIAN TEA

1 c. Tang
1 t. cinnamon
¼ c. instant tea
½ t. cloves
½ pkg. lemonade mix with sugar

Mix all ingredients together and keep in a tightly sealed jar. Use 1½ teaspoonsful in a teacup of hot water or 2 heaping teaspoonsful in a mug.

SKINNY MARY

¾ c. tomato juice
1 T. Worcestershire sauce
¼ c. sauerkraut juice
Ice cubes

Pour tomato and sauerkraut juice over ice cubes in glass. Add Worcestershire sauce and stir. Serve at once. Makes 1 serving.

LEMONADE

½ c. lemon juice (2 lemons)
3 c. cold water
½ c. sugar
Ice cubes

Add sugar to juice. Stir in cold water. Pour over ice in glasses. For hot lemonade, use hot water instead of cold.

Note: Roll lemons on table to make more juice.

Salads and Dressings

STUFFED PRUNE SALAD

12 large cooked prunes
2 3-oz. pkgs. cream cheese
2 c. grapefruit sections
¼ c. mayonnaise
¼ c. chopped nuts
Lettuce

Drain prunes and remove the pits. Blend cream cheese and mayonnaise; fill centers of prunes. Sprinkle with nuts. Arrange on lettuce leaves with grapefruit sections and serve with a salad dressing of your choice. Serves 4.

GERMAN POTATO SALAD

¼ c. sugar
1 T. flour
2 t. salt
¼ t. pepper
¼ c. vinegar
⅔ c. water
4 slices bacon, diced and browned
¼ c. bacon drippings
4 c. cold, cooked, cubed potatoes
1 hard-boiled egg
2 T. chopped onion
Sprig parsley

Combine sugar, flour, salt and pepper in the top of a double boiler. Stir in vinegar, water, bacon and bacon drippings. Cook, stirring constantly, about 5 minutes, or until thick. Place potatoes, onions, egg and parsley in a greased casserole or baking pan. Pour dressing over and mix to coat all. Heat in a 350° oven for 30 minutes. Serves 6 to 8.

PERFECTION SALAD

2 T. unflavored gelatin
2½ c. cold water
1 c. boiling water
⅓ c. sugar
1 t. salt
¼ c. tarragon vinegar
2½ T. lemon juice
½ t. prepared horseradish
3 carrots, grated
1 c. thinly sliced celery
1 2-oz. jar diced pimiento
2 c. finely shredded cabbage
½ green pepper, chopped
2 green onions and tops, thinly sliced

Soften gelatin in ½ cup cold water. Stir in boiling water, sugar and salt. Stir until dissolved. If necessary, place over low heat to dissolve. Add remaining 2 cups cold water, vinegar, lemon juice, and horseradish. Chill to a soft set. Fold in remaining ingredients. Turn into a 6-cup mold. Chill overnight. Unmold to serve. Serves 6.

CELEBRATION SALAD

2 c. diced cooked chicken
2 c. diced cooked ham
2 c. diced celery
1 c. salted almonds
½ c. mayonnaise
1 hard-boiled egg
2 T. pimiento slices
Lettuce

Combine chicken, ham, celery, almonds and mayonnaise. Serve on lettuce leaves. Cut egg lengthwise into eighths. Garnish salad with egg wedges and pimiento. Serve with hot biscuits. Serves 6.

Pictured opposite
Celebration Salad
(page 6)

FROSTED FRUIT SALAD

1 3-oz. pkg. lemon gelatin
1 3-oz. pkg. orange gelatin
  Juice of 1 lemon
2 c. boiling water
2 c. cold water
2 bananas, diced
1 No. 2 can crushed pineapple, drained
1 c. minature marshmallows

Dissolve gelatin in boiling water. Add cold water and lemon juice. Chill until partly set. Fold in pineapple, marshmallows and bananas. Pour into a 9 x 12 x 3-inch loaf pan. Chill until set. When gelatin is firm frost with Frosting. Serves 8.

Frosting

2 T. flour
½ c. sugar
1 egg, beaten
½ c. milk
1 c. pineapple juice
1 c. heavy cream, whipped

Combine flour and sugar. Slowly stir in egg and milk. Stir in pineapple juice. Cook, stirring constantly, until thickened. Cool. Fold in whipped cream.

HAM SALAD

1 3-oz. pkg. lemon gelatin
1⅔ c. boiling water
1 T. lemon juice
¼ t. salt
1 c. chopped, cooked ham
¼ c. chopped celery
2 T. chopped green pepper
½ t. chopped onion
2 T. chopped pimiento

Dissolve gelatin in boiling water; add lemon juice and salt. Cool until slightly thickened. Pour half the gelatin into individual molds or one large mold, filling molds only half full. Chill just until set. Stir ham and vegetables into remaining gelatin and gently pour on top of set gelatin. Refrigerate until completely set. Unmold on rings of pineapple or garnish with pineapple. Serves 8.

JELLIED BEET SALAD

1 3-oz. pkg. lemon or lime gelatin
1 c. boiling water
1 c. cold beet juice
3 T. vinegar
2 T. minced onion
1 T. horseradish
¾ c. celery
1 16-oz. can diced beets, drained

Dissolve gelatin in boiling water. Stir in beet juice and vinegar. Add onion, horseradish, celery and diced beets. Refrigerate overnight. Serve on a bed of lettuce. Serves 4.

POTATO SALAD

4 c. potatoes, cooked and diced
6 hard-boiled eggs, chopped
½ c. chopped green pepper
2 T. chopped ripe olives
1½ to 2 c. mayonnaise
1 t. salt
1 c. diced celery
½ c. diced pimiento
1 large onion, chopped
  Paprika

Mix together all ingredients, stirring thoroughly to coat all with mayonnaise. Place in serving dish. Sprinkle with paprika. Refrigerate until serving time. Serves 6.

THREE BEAN SALAD

1 16-oz. can green beans
1 16-oz. can wax beans
1 16-oz. can kidney beans
½ c. sugar
½ c. vinegar
½ t. celery seed
1 T. vegetable oil
1 medium onion, chopped

Combine beans. Slowly stir vinegar into sugar, blending until smooth. Add celery seed, oil and onion. Refrigerate.

SEA SALAD SURPRISE

2 c. tuna fish
1 c. lobster meat
2 c. shrimp, cooked and deveined
1 lemon, cut in wedges
2 c. diced celery
¾ c. mayonnaise
1 bunch watercress

Clean and slice fish. Reserve 12 whole shrimp for garnish. Combine all with mayonnaise and serve on watercress. Garnish with whole shrimp and lemon wedges. Serve with hot hard rolls. Serves 6.

MOLDED CRANBERRY SALAD

1 16-oz. can whole cranberry sauce
1 c. boiling water
1 3-oz. pkg. strawberry gelatin
1 T. lemon juice
¼ t. salt
½ c. mayonnaise
1 apple, diced
½ c. finely chopped celery
¼ c. chopped nuts

Heat cranberry sauce. Strain. Mix cranberry liquid, boiling water and gelatin, stirring until gelatin is dissolved. Add lemon juice and salt. Chill mixture until slightly thickened. Stir in mayonnaise; beat until fluffy. Fold in reserved cranberries, apple, celery and nuts. Pour into a mold or a flat pan; cut in squares to serve. Refrigerate until firm. Makes 6 servings.

FRENCH DRESSING

¼ c. vegetable oil
1 T. sugar
½ t. pepper
2 T. cider vinegar
1 t. salt
½ t. paprika

Place all ingredients in a pint jar; shake vigorously until thick. Serves 4.

LO-CAL TOMATO JUICE DRESSING

½ c. canned tomato juice
2 T. lemon juice or vinegar
1 t. salt
1½ T. Worcestershire sauce
2 to 4 T. vegetable oil
½ t. dry mustard
1 t. minced onion
3 T. sugar substitute

Combine all ingredients and beat until well blended. Makes 1 cup. Contains 25 calories per tablespoon.

BOILED SALAD DRESSING

2 T. flour
1 t. salt
¾ t. dry mustard
1 T. sugar
⅛ t. pepper
½ t. paprika
1 egg, slightly beaten
1 c. milk
¼ c. cider vinegar
2 T. butter or margarine

In the top of a double boiler, mix together flour, salt, mustard, sugar, pepper and paprika. Gradually stir in egg and milk. Cook over boiling water, stirring constantly, until thick. Add vinegar and butter. Cool. Makes 1⅔ cups.

NEW ORLEANS DRESSING

½ t. salt
½ t. dry mustard
¼ c. vinegar
¼ t. sugar
¾ c. vegetable oil
¼ t. pepper

Combine all ingredients in a screw-top jar. Shake vigorously. Rub bowl with clove of garlic before tossing green salad with dressing.

CELERY SEED DRESSING

2½ c. sugar
4 t. dry mustard
4 t. salt
1¼ c. vinegar
1 small onion, grated
4 c. vegetable oil
¼ c. celery seed

Combine sugar, mustard and salt. Add half the vinegar and onion to dry mixture. Beat on medium speed of mixer for 15 minutes. Stir in oil, then remainder of vinegar. Mix until well blended. Fold in celery seed. Refrigerate. Makes 3 pints.

ROQUEFORT CHEESE DRESSING

1 t. salt
1 t. celery seed
1 t. paprika
1 t. dry mustard
1 t. minced onion
4 T. sugar
¼ c. grated Roquefort cheese
⅔ c. vegetable oil
4 T. lemon juice

Mix dry ingredients together. Blend with a little of the oil. Stir in remaining oil, alternating with lemon juice. When ready to serve, add cheese.

MAYONNAISE

2 egg yolks
1 t. salt
1 t. dry mustard
2 c. vegetable oil
2 T. lemon juice or vinegar

Beat egg yolks, salt and mustard until light and lemon colored. Add oil, a small amount at a time. Beat until mixture is emulsified. Stir in lemon juice or vinegar. Refrigerate until needed. Makes 1 pint.

MRS. SMITH'S SALAD DRESSING

3 whole eggs, slightly beaten
1 T. flour, rounded
¾ t. salt
2 T. butter
⅓ c. sugar
½ t. dry mustard
½ c. cider vinegar

Mix all ingredients in top of a double boiler. Cook over boiling water, stirring constantly, until thick and smooth. Cool.

FRENCH DRESSING

1 10¾-oz. can tomato soup
1 c. sugar
1 c. cider vinegar
1 c. vegetable oil
2 T. Worcestershire sauce
1 t. salt
1 t. dry mustard
1 t. paprika
1 t. dry onion flakes *or* 1 T. minced onion

Place all ingredients in a screw-top jar. Shake well. Store in refrigerator. Makes 1 quart.

Pictured opposite
from left
Mrs. Smith's Salad Dressing
Russian Dressing
Roquefort Cheese Dressing (on salad)
(page 11)

RUSSIAN DRESSING

¼ c. white corn syrup
½ t. salt
½ t. celery seed
1 T. vinegar
1 T. Worcestershire sauce
1 medium onion, finely chopped
⅓ c. sugar
½ t. paprika
2 T. lemon juice
½ c. catsup
1 c. salad oil

Combine all ingredients in a screw-top jar. Shake well. Refrigerate.

Vegetable Dishes

FRIED GREEN TOMATOES

4 medium-size green tomatoes
1 t. salt
½ c. flour
2 T. vegetable oil

Wash and slice green tomatoes in ½-inch thick slices. Sprinkle with salt. Roll each slice in flour until coated on each side. Place oil in a skillet and heat. Place floured tomato slices in skillet. Fry over low heat until browned on both sides. Serve hot. Serves 4.

STUFFED CUCUMBER

1 large cucumber
2 3-oz. pkgs. cream cheese
1 T. chopped pimiento
3 T. mayonnaise
1 T. chopped stuffed olives
1 T. chopped ripe olives
Lettuce leaves

Cut cucumber in half lengthwise. With a spoon scoop out seeds and membrane. Soften cream cheese with mayonnaise. Mix in olives and pimiento. Fill the cucumber cavity with the cream cheese mixture until level. Press cucumber halves together. Refrigerate for at least 2 hours. To serve, slice thin and place on lettuce leaf. Serve with Roquefort cheese dressing.

GLAZED PARSNIPS

3 c. parsnips, sliced diagonally in ½-inch slices
¾ c. boiling water
½ t. salt
2 T. butter
¼ c. orange juice
1 t. grated orange rind

Place parsnips in water with salt. Bring to a boil. Simmer, covered, about 20 minutes. Drain. Heat remaining ingredients together in a saucepan. Pour over parsnips in serving dish. Serves 6.

SPINACH BALLS

2 c. chopped spinach, cooked and drained
2 T. grated cheese
2 T. melted butter
1½ c. bread crumbs
2 eggs
¼ c. water
⅓ t. pepper
½ t. salt
¼ c. margarine
Bread crumbs

Combine spinach, cheese, butter, bread crumbs and 1 beaten egg. Roll into balls. To other egg, add water and seasoning and beat. Dip spinach balls into additional bread crumbs, then into egg mixture, and again in bread crumbs. Brown balls on both sides in margarine. Serves 4.

POTATO CROQUETTES

2 c. mashed potatoes
1 egg
1 t. salt
¼ t. black pepper
2 T. chopped parsley
1 T. Parmesan cheese
1 clove garlic, minced (optional)
¾ c. bread crumbs
1 egg, beaten
1 T. water

Thoroughly mix potatoes, 1 egg, salt, pepper, parsley, cheese and garlic, if desired. Shape into small balls. Dip balls in bread crumbs, then into egg mixed with water, and again in the bread crumbs. Let stand on waxed paper 20 minutes. Fry in deep fat until browned on all sides. Serves 4.

POLENTA

3 c. water
1½ t. salt
1 c. yellow cornmeal
1 c. cold water
2 T. vegetable oil
1 lb. Italian sausage, casings removed
1 lb. mushrooms, cleaned and
   sliced lengthwise
2½ c. tomatoes
1 t. salt
¼ t. pepper
½ c. grated Parmesan or Romano cheese

Bring water and salt to a boil. Mix cornmeal with cold water; gradually stir into boiling water. Continue boiling, stirring constantly, until mixture thickens. Cover; lower heat. Simmer 10 minutes. Meanwhile, to make sauce, place oil in heavy skillet. Crumble sausages in skillet; add mushrooms. Cook until mushrooms and sausages are lightly browned. Stir in tomatoes, salt and pepper; simmer 20 to 30 minutes. To serve, transfer cooked cornmeal to a warm platter. Top with tomato sauce and sprinkle with grated Parmesan or Romano cheese. Serves 6 to 8.

SAUERKRAUT STUFFING FOR GOOSE

2½ lbs. sauerkraut
1 grated carrot
1 c. salami or other sausage
1 T. goose or bacon fat
1 potato, grated
1 onion, minced
½ c. dried bread crumbs

Mix all ingredients together. Stuff into goose that has been prepared for roasting. Sew up. Place in roasting pan. Roast, uncovered, in a 350° oven for 2 hours or until goose is done. Pour off fat occasionally.

MAPLE-GLAZED SQUASH AND PARSNIPS

8 parsnips (1½ lbs.)
2 small acorn squash
1¼ c. maple syrup
   Water
1 t. salt
3 T. butter or margarine
1 T. chopped parsley
¼ t. nutmeg

Pare parsnips; cut in quarters, lengthwise then crosswise into thirds. Halve squash crosswise; scoop out seeds and stringy membrane. Cut squash into ½-inch slices. Do not peel. Cook parsnips and squash in a large skillet in boiling salted water for 10 minutes or until almost tender. Drain. Heat maple syrup in same skillet. Add butter or margarine. Stir until melted. Return parsnips and squash to skillet. Simmer over medium heat, basting frequently, until vegetables are tender and glazed. Remove squash with slotted spoon. Arrange slices around edges of heated platter. Spoon parsnips into the center. Drizzle remaining syrup over vegetables. Sprinkle with parsley and nutmeg. Serves 8.

STUFFED CABBAGE LEAVES

12 large cabbage leaves
1 lb. ground beef
1 c. cooked rice
⅔ c. milk
1 egg
¼ c. onion, finely chopped
1 t. chopped parsley
1 t. salt
½ t. sage
2 T. brown sugar
⅔ c. water
4 whole cloves
1 10½-oz. can condensed tomato soup

Drop cabbage leaves into boiling water. Boil for 5 minutes; drain. Cut thick vein from each leaf. Brown ground beef. Mix beef, rice, milk, egg, 2 tablespoons of the onion, parsley, salt and sage. Place a spoonful on each leaf. Roll up the leaf and secure with a toothpick. Place rolls in a buttered 13 x 9 x 2-inch pan. Sprinkle with brown sugar. Mix the remaining onion with soup, water and cloves. Pour over cabbage rolls. Bake uncovered in a 325° oven for 1½ hours. Serves 6.

RED CABBAGE

3 strips bacon
1½ lbs. red cabbage
1 medium onion, finely chopped
7 bay leaves
2 T. mixed pickling spice
3 T. honey *or* sugar
  Juice of 2 lemons *or* ¼ c. vinegar
½ t. salt
⅛ t. pepper

Fry bacon until crisp. Remove from pan and break into small pieces. Shred cabbage leaves in ¼-inch wide strips. Add to bacon grease along with crumbled bacon. Cover tightly and simmer for 20 minutes. Add onion, bay leaves and pickling spice, tied in cheesecloth. Stir in honey, lemon juice or vinegar. Cover and simmer slowly for about 1½ hours. Add salt and pepper and steam ½ hour. Serves 4.

Pictured opposite
Red Cabbage (page 15)
with a pork roast and potatoes

CORN AND TOMATOES

6 large, fresh tomatoes
2 c. fresh corn
½ t. salt
1 t. chopped chives
½ t. pepper
¼ t. sweet basil

Pour boiling water over tomatoes. Cool slightly; slip off tomato skins. Chop tomatoes. Combine corn and tomatoes in a saucepan. Add salt, pepper, chives and basil. Simmer over low heat for 20 minutes or until vegetables are tender. Serves 6.

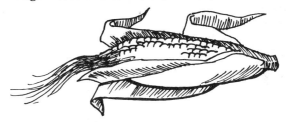

STUFFED GREEN PEPPERS

4 large green peppers
1 lb. ground beef
¼ c. vegetable oil
½ t. salt
¼ t. pepper
1 T. minced parsley
⅔ c. cooked rice
1½ c. tomatoes, sieved
¼ c. minced onion
½ t. salt
¼ c. water
¼ t. pepper
2 slices mozzarella cheese

Grease a 2-quart baking dish. Rinse peppers. Cut a thin slice from the stem end of each green pepper and remove inner white fiber and seeds. Rinse cavity. Drop peppers in boiling salted water to cover. Simmer for 5 minutes. Remove and set aside to drain. Brown ground beef in oil. Stir in parsley, salt, pepper and cooked rice. Lightly fill pepper shells with the mixture, heaping slightly. Place in a baking dish. Combine tomatoes, onion, salt, water and pepper, mixing well. Pour over peppers. Place a strip of cheese on top of each pepper. Bake in a 350° oven for 30 minutes. Serves 4.

EGGPLANT WITH SHRIMP OR HAM FILLING

1 1½ to 2-lb. eggplant
2 T. butter or margarine
¼ c. chopped onion
2 T. chopped green pepper
1 clove garlic, minced
2 c. shrimp or ham
1 c. soft bread crumbs
2 T. pimiento, chopped
½ t. salt
¼ t. pepper
1 c. Buttered Bread Crumbs

Split eggplant in half lengthwise. Cook, covered, in a small amount of boiling water for 10 minutes or until slightly tender. Remove from water and drain. Scoop out pulp from center of eggplant, leaving ¼-inch shell. Set shells aside. Finely chop the pulp. Melt butter; add pulp, onion, green pepper and garlic. Sauté until onion is transparent. Chop shrimp or ham. Add shrimp, bread crumbs, pimiento, salt and pepper to onion mixture. Blend thoroughly. Spoon mixture into eggplant shells, heaping slightly. Cover tops with buttered bread crumbs. Bake in a 375° oven for 20 to 30 minutes or until crumbs are browned. Serves 6 to 8.

BUTTERED BREAD CRUMBS

2 T. melted butter
1 c. soft bread crumbs

Melt butter. Add bread crumbs and sauté until slightly browned.

PAPRIKA BROWNED POTATOES

2 c. boiled potatoes, thinly sliced
3 T. margarine
¼ t. pepper
½ t. salt
1 t. paprika

Melt margarine in a heavy skillet. Add potatoes, salt, pepper and paprika. Mix well and brown lightly over low heat until potatoes are warmed through and reddish brown in color. Serves 4.

BAKED STUFFED TOMATOES

2 T. vegetable oil
1 t. chopped onion
¼ c. ground beef
½ c. grated cheese
1 t. salt
1 c. cooked rice
6 large ripe tomatoes

Grease an 8 x 8 x 2-inch baking dish. Heat oil in skillet; brown onion and ground beef. Stir in cheese, seasonings and rice. Set aside. With a sharp knife, cut a ¼-inch slice from top of each tomato. Cut around inside of tomatoes, being careful not to cut through the bottom. Scoop out center pulp. Sieve the tomato pulp and set aside the liquid. Sprinkle each tomato with salt. Lightly fill the tomatoes with filling. Place tomatoes in baking dish. Pour the tomato juice over tomatoes. Bake in a 375° oven for 20 to 25 minutes. Garnish with parsley. Serves 6.

STUFFED GRAPE LEAVES

12 large grape leaves
½ lb. ground beef
1 medium onion, minced
2 T. vegetable oil
1 T. grated lemon rind
1 t. salt
⅛ t. pepper
½ c. white raisins
2 c. cooked rice

Grease a 1½-quart casserole. Wash grape leaves. Blanch the grape leaves in boiling water for 30 seconds. Drain. Plunge in cold water; drain and set aside. Brown ground beef and onion in oil. Stir in lemon rind, salt, pepper, raisins and rice. Place one-third cup filling on each grape leaf. Fold leaves around the filling. Place in the casserole with folded side down. Continue until all grape leaves and filling are gone. Add 1 cup water. Cover and bake in a 350° oven 20 to 30 minutes until liquid is almost gone. Serves 4.

GREEN BEAN CASSEROLE

3 6-oz. pkgs. frozen green
  beans, French cut
1 8-oz. can water chestnuts
½ c. butter
4 green onions *or* 1 medium onion,
  chopped
2 4-oz. cans mushrooms
½ c. flour
2 c. milk
¾ c. shredded Cheddar cheese
2 t. soy sauce
½ t. Tabasco sauce
1 t. salt
¾ c. slivered almonds

Cook frozen beans according to package directions. Drain. Chop water chestnuts and add to beans. Sauté onion and mushrooms in butter. Stir in flour, milk and cheese. Cook over low heat until thickened, stirring occasionally. Stir in soy sauce, Tabasco sauce and salt. Pour sauce over beans and mix gently. Turn into a 2-quart buttered casserole. Sprinkle almonds over top. Bake for 20 minutes in a 375° oven. Serves 8 to 10.

SCALLOPED POTATOES

3 or 4 large white potatoes, thinly sliced
1 small onion, sliced
½ t. pepper
1 t. salt
⅓ c. flour
½ c. bread crumbs
2 c. milk or more
4 to 5 T. butter or margarine

Grease a 2-quart casserole. Alternate layers of sliced potatoes and onion. Sprinkle each layer with salt, pepper and flour. Dot with butter. Repeat until casserole is full. Pour milk over, barely covering potatoes. Sprinkle top with bread crumbs and dot with additional butter. Bake in a 375° oven 45 to 60 minutes or until potatoes are tender. Serves 4.

LEFSE

1 T. melted butter
1 T. sugar
¼ t. salt
1 c. cream
10 c. mashed potatoes
  Flour

Add butter, sugar, salt and cream to mashed potatoes. Blend well. Add enough flour to handle without being sticky. Dough will be similar to pie dough. Cool completely and roll very thin in 8 to 9-inch circles. (To prevent sticking, dough must be rolled with a covered rolling pin.) Bake dough on *lefse* grill or pancake grill. Turn only once when underside is brown spotted. Makes about 35 circles. To serve, cut circles into wedges. Butter and roll up. The *lefse* pieces were traditionally used to wrap around a piece of fish or meat before eating. Serves 8 to 10.

BAKED FILLED SWEET POTATOES

6 medium-size yams
1 T. shortening
12 pork sausage links
½ c. hot orange juice
3 T. butter or margarine
2 T. brown sugar
1 t. grated orange peel
1 t. salt
½ t. nutmeg

Rub potato skins with shortening. Bake in a 450° oven for 45 to 60 minutes. While potatoes are baking, pan broil pork sausage links. Drain on paper towels and keep warm. When sweet potatoes are tender, cut each potato in half lengthwise. Scoop out inside of the potato without breaking skin. Mash or rice potato; whip in hot orange juice, butter, brown sugar, orange peel, salt and nutmeg. Pile mixture lightly into potato shells. Top each with 2 sausage links. Bake in a 350° oven 8 to 10 minutes longer, or until potatoes are reheated and browned lightly. Serves 6.

BLUSHING CAULIFLOWER

1 head cauliflower
½ t. salt
2 T. butter
1 clove garlic, crushed
1 10-oz. can condensed tomato soup
½ c. grated American cheese
1 T. chopped parsley

Place cauliflower in a large kettle. Add salted water to cover bottom of the pan. Simmer over low heat for about 20 to 30 minutes, or until tender. Melt butter in a saucepan. Sauté garlic until lightly browned. Add soup and cheese; heat, stirring occasionally, over low heat until cheese is melted. Pour sauce over cauliflower; sprinkle with parsley. Serves 6.

POTATO CAKES

6 large potatoes
¼ c. milk
3 eggs, beaten
½ t. salt
3 T. butter
1 t. baking powder
2 c. flour
Cream Sauce

Peel and boil potatoes in salted water until tender. Drain and mash. Beat in milk, eggs, salt, flour and baking powder. Form into patties. Brown potato patties lightly in hot butter. Serve with Cream Sauce. Serves 6.

CREAM SAUCE

4 c. milk, heated
3 T. flour
⅓ c. sugar
¼ c. cold milk
2 T. butter
1 t. caraway seed

Heat milk in saucepan. Mix flour and sugar with the cold milk. Stir into hot milk, stirring until mixture boils and thickens. Add butter and caraway seed, stirring to melt butter.

BAKED STUFFED MUSHROOMS

1 lb. mushrooms with 1 to 2-inch caps
2 T. vegetable oil
¼ c. chopped onion
⅓ c. bread crumbs
3 T. grated Parmesan cheese
1 T. chopped parsley
½ t. salt
⅛ t. oregano
2 T. vegetable oil

Clean mushrooms; remove stems. Place caps, open side up, in a greased 1½-quart casserole. Set aside. Finely chop mushroom stems. In a skillet heat oil; add mushroom stems and onion. Sauté over low heat until onion is lightly browned. Combine bread crumbs, cheese, parsley, salt and oregano. Add to mushroom stems and onions. Pile mixture lightly into mushroom caps. Drizzle remaining oil over caps. Bake in a 400° oven for 15 to 20 minutes or until mushrooms are tender and tops are browned. Serves 6 to 8.

EGGPLANT PARMIGIANA

2 medium-size eggplants
1 c. vegetable oil
2 6-oz. cans tomato paste
2 c. water
½ c. grated Parmesan cheese
1 3-oz. can mushrooms
1 lb. mozzarella cheese

Peel eggplant and slice into ½-inch slices. Fry in oil until lightly browned. Drain on paper towels. Cover bottom of a 13 x 9 x 2-inch buttered pan with a layer of eggplant slices. Combine tomato paste and water, mixing well. Pour over eggplant. Sprinkle with Parmesan cheese, mushrooms and mozzarella cheese. Repeat layers, ending with mozzarella cheese. Bake in a 400° oven for 20 minutes or until cheese is bubbly. Makes 10 servings.

Pictured opposite
Baked Stuffed Onions
(page 19)

BAKED STUFFED ONIONS

6 large onions
½ t. salt
2 T. vegetable oil
¼ lb. ground beef
1 c. cooked rice
1 egg yolk
½ c. soft bread crumbs
½ t. salt
½ t. pepper
2 T. melted butter
2 T. grated Parmesan cheese
½ c. soft bread crumbs
1 T. chopped parsley

Cut off root; peel and rinse onions. Cut a ½-inch slice from the top of each onion. Cook onion, uncovered, in salted water to cover for 10 to 15 minutes or until slightly tender. Drain well; cool. Heat oil in skillet; add ground beef and sauté until browned. Scoop centers out of onions; chop and add to ground beef. Sauté until golden. Combine rice, egg yolk, salt, pepper and bread crumbs with meat mixture. Fill onions. Mix together melted butter, cheese, parsley and bread crumbs. Spread over top of onions. Bake in a greased casserole in a 350° oven for 1 hour. Serves 6.

FRIED ZUCCHINI WITH ONIONS

2 T. margarine
2 medium-size onions, sliced
1 fresh zucchini squash
1 t. salt
¼ t. pepper
¼ c. water

In a heavy skillet, melt margarine; lightly sauté onion slices. Wash zucchini; slice in thin rounds, leaving skin on. Add to onion with salt and pepper. Fry over low heat, turning as slices brown. Add water and lower heat. Cover tightly and steam for 20 to 25 minutes, stirring occasionally, until tender. Serves 4.

FRIED PARSNIPS

6 to 8 parsnips (1½ lbs.)
½ t. salt
3 T. butter

Pare parsnips. Cut in half lengthwise and then in half crosswise. Put in kettle with water to cover; add salt. Cook until tender; drain. Melt butter in skillet. Arrange parsnips in one layer in skillet. Brown on all sides, turning to keep from burning. Serves 8. Can use carrots this way, too.

CARROTS AND CELERY

2 c. diced celery
4 to 6 carrots, diced
½ t. salt
Water
2 T. melted butter
1 t. chopped parsley

Place celery and carrots in a saucepan with enough salted water to cover. Simmer over low heat 30 minutes or until carrots and celery are tender. Drain. Pour into a serving dish. Pour melted butter over carrots and sprinkle with parsley. Serves 4.

POTATO DUMPLINGS

6 large potatoes, boiled and mashed
1 c. flour
1 t. salt
½ t. nutmeg
3 eggs, beaten slightly
½ lb. ground beef

To cooled potatoes, add flour, salt, nutmeg and eggs. Roll ground beef into balls, ½ inch in diameter. Mold potato mixture around meatballs. Drop in boiling water. Cover tightly and continue boiling for 15 minutes. Do not lift lid. Serve with vegetable soup. Serves 6.

HONEYED SWEET POTATOES

1½ lbs. sweet potatoes
⅓ c. butter
⅔ c. honey
Salted water

Scrub sweet potatoes and cut into quarters. Place in a stewing kettle. Cover with salted water and boil until almost done, about 30 minutes. Drain; cool slightly. Remove skins and slice crosswise in ½-inch slices. Place in a 1½-quart buttered casserole. Mix honey and butter together. Bake in a 350° oven for 20 to 25 minutes or until lightly browned. Serve at once. Serves 4 to 6.

SOUTHERN CORN PUDDING

2 eggs
2 c. fresh corn
2 c. milk
½ t. salt
½ t. pepper
1 T. vegetable oil

Beat eggs until light. Add milk, corn, seasonings and oil in a large mixing bowl. Mix well. Turn into a 1-quart buttered casserole. Bake in a 350° oven for 30 minutes. Serves 6.

CUCUMBERS IN SOUR CREAM

3 medium-size cucumbers
½ c. sour cream
2 T. cider vinegar
1 t. sugar
½ t. salt
½ t. black pepper

Peel cucumbers and slice thin. Layer cucumbers in a medium-size bowl. Cover with 3 cups water, or enough to cover, and 1½ teaspoon salt. Chill. Pour off salted water and rinse in clear water. Drain. Blend sour cream, vinegar, and sugar. Fold into cucumbers. Serve with a sprinkling of salt and pepper.

STEWED SAUERKRAUT

1 30-oz. can sauerkraut
3 T. caraway seed
1 c. water
1 medium onion, sliced
¼ c. sugar
1 medium potato, grated

Mix all ingredients except potato in a saucepan. Let simmer, stirring occasionally, until onion is soft and transparent. Stir in potato. Just bring mixture to a boil; cover. Let stand for 10 minutes before serving. Serves 4 to 6.

SKILLET SALAD

4 slices bacon
¼ c. vinegar
1 T. brown sugar
1 t. salt
1 T. finely chopped onion
4 c. shredded cabbage
¼ c. chopped parsley

Cook bacon until crisp; drain and crumble. To fat in skillet, add vinegar, sugar, salt and onion. Bring to a boil. Remove from heat; toss cabbage and parsley in hot mixture. Makes 6 servings.

BROCCOLI PARMESAN

1 bunch fresh broccoli
2 T. butter
2 T. minced onion
¼ t. pepper
½ t. dry mustard
½ c. grated Parmesan cheese
½ t. salt
¼ t. marjoram
3 T. flour
1 chicken bouillon cube
2½ c. milk
2 T. grated Parmesan cheese
1 t. paprika

Cook broccoli in boiling salted water until tender. Drain. Arrange broccoli in a shallow greased baking dish. Melt butter in a saucepan. Add onion and sauté over low heat until tender. Blend in seasonings and flour. Add bouillon cube and milk. Cook over medium heat, stirring constantly, until mixture thickens and comes to a boil. Add cheese and stir well, until melted. Pour sauce over broccoli. Sprinkle with paprika and additional Parmesan cheese. Bake in a 375° oven for 20 to 25 minutes or until browned. Serves 4 to 6.

RAW FRIED POTATOES

6 to 8 medium-size potatoes, peeled and thinly sliced
3 T. shortening
1 t. salt
½ t. pepper
1 c. chopped onion, optional
¼ c. water

Heat shortening in large skillet. Add sliced potatoes, salt and pepper and onion, if desired. Fry on medium-low heat, stirring potatoes up from the bottom as they brown. Fry about 15 minutes. Add water and cover tightly. Cook over low heat until potatoes are tender, stirring occasionally. Serves 4 to 6.

HOT COLE SLAW

½ c. cider vinegar
¼ c. water
½ t. salt
¼ c. sugar
¼ t. paprika
¼ t. dry mustard
¼ c. vegetable oil
¼ c. heavy cream
2 eggs, slightly beaten
1 head cabbage, shredded fine
½ c. pickle relish
1 2-oz. jar pimiento, diced

Place vinegar, water, salt, sugar, paprika, mustard and oil in a pan and bring to a boil. Remove from heat. Combine eggs and cream. Stir a little of the hot mixture into egg-cream mixture. Continue stirring and slowly pour remaining hot mixture into the egg mixture. Return to pan and cook on low heat for 5 minutes, stirring constantly. Mix together cabbage, pimiento and pickle relish. Pour hot dressing over and toss lightly. Serve immediately. Serves 8.

BROCCOLI CUSTARD

1 bunch broccoli
½ lb. fresh mushrooms
3 T. butter
1 c. grated Cheddar cheese
3 eggs, well beaten
1 10¾-oz. can condensed cream of celery soup
⅓ c. milk
1 t. grated onion
½ t. salt
1 t. Worcestershire sauce
¼ t. pepper
⅓ c. French bread crumbs

Trim and wash broccoli. Cook until barely tender. Drain and set aside. Sauté whole mushrooms in butter. Arrange broccoli and mushrooms in a shallow, greased 1½-quart baking dish. Combine ½ cup of the cheese, eggs, soup, milk and seasonings. Pour over the vegetables. Sprinkle with remaining cheese and bread crumbs. Set dish in shallow pan of water. Bake in a 350° oven for 45 minutes, or until custard is set. Serves 6.

CORN PUDDING

3 eggs, beaten
1 c. milk
2 c. corn
3 T. chopped green pepper
1 t. grated onion
1 T. minced parsley
½ t. salt
¼ t. pepper

In a large mixing bowl, combine eggs and milk; mix well. Add corn, green pepper, onion, parsley and seasonings. Turn into a buttered 1½-quart casserole. Bake in a 350° oven for 1 hour or until firm. Serves 6.

STUFFED ZUCCHINI

4 zucchini squash
1 green pepper, diced
1 small onion, chopped
1 T. butter
½ lb. ground beef
2 c. fresh corn
1 tomato, chopped
1 pimiento, diced
1 egg, slightly beaten
1 c. bread crumbs
1 T. Worcestershire sauce
¼ t. pepper
1 t. salt

Split zucchini in halves lengthwise and scoop out seeds and membrane. Set aside. Sauté green pepper and onion in butter until onion is transparent. Remove and set aside. Brown ground beef, separating with a fork. Add green pepper, onion and remaining ingredients. Place zucchini halves in a well-greased baking pan. Fill each half with corn stuffing. Pour one-half cup water in the bottom of the pan; cover with foil. Bake in a 350° oven until zucchini is tender. Remove foil and bake an additional ½ hour. Serves 6 to 8.

Pictured opposite
Stuffed Zucchini
(page 22)

SQUAW CORN

2 c. whole kernel corn
2 T. margarine
1 green pepper, diced
2 medium onions, chopped
1 small jar pimiento, diced
¼ t. pepper

Melt margarine in skillet. Add green pepper and onion. Sauté slowly over low heat until tender and onion is transparent. Add drained corn, pimiento and seasonings. Cook over low heat for 20 minutes. Serve in a warm bowl. Serves 4.

CARROTS SUPREME

4 c. carrots, chopped
½ t. salt
  Water
½ lb. bacon, diced
1 medium onion, diced
¼ t. pepper

Cook carrots in boiling, salted water until tender. Drain and set aside. Brown bacon in skillet. Drain and set aside. Sauté onion in bacon fat. Remove to dish. Mash carrots with potato masher; stir in bacon, onions, drippings and seasoning. Mix well. Serve hot. Serves 4.

BUTTERED PARSNIPS

8 parsnips (1½ lbs.)
½ t. salt
2 T. melted butter
2 T. parsley, chopped

Pare the parsnips and quarter. Split in half lengthwise. Place in a kettle with salted water to cover. Simmer until tender; drain. Pour melted butter over parsnips in serving dish. Mix to coat all sides. Sprinkle with parsley and serve. Serves 6.

VEGETABLE DISH

2 16-oz. cans green beans
2 16-oz. cans small, whole onions
2 16-oz. cans potatoes
1 16-oz. can small carrot pieces
2 2½-oz. jars mushrooms
1 head cauliflower, broken into flowerets
½ t. salt
½ t. pepper
  Paprika
  Cheese Sauce

Drain all vegetables and combine in a buttered 9 x 13 x 2-inch baking dish. Stir in Cheese Sauce and sprinkle top with paprika. Bake in a 350° oven for 1 hour. Serves 6.

CHEESE SAUCE

4 T. butter
4 T. flour
2 c. milk
1 t. salt
¼ t. pepper
½ lb. Cheddar cheese

Melt butter in saucepan. Add flour, salt and pepper. Gradually stir in milk. Simmer 2 to 3 minutes, or until thickened. Add cheese, stirring to melt. Blend thoroughly.

PEAS AND CARROTS

1 10-oz. pkg. frozen peas *or* 2 c. fresh peas
4 carrots, diced
2 c. water
½ t. salt
2 T. melted butter *or* 2 c. White Sauce

Cook peas and carrots in salted water until carrots are tender, about 15 minutes. Drain. Add melted butter or White Sauce. Serve hot. Serves 8.

WHITE SAUCE

2 T. butter
2 T. flour
2 c. milk

Melt butter in saucepan; add flour. Stir in milk and cook, stirring, until thick.

SNOW PEAS

4 c. fresh snow peas *or* 2 6-oz. pkgs.
  frozen snow peas
2 c. water
½ t. salt
2 T. melted butter

Prepare fresh snow peas by breaking off tips and tails. Wash and place in saucepan in salted water. Drain. Drop frozen snow peas in boiling salted water and cook until tender. Drain. Add melted butter and serve. Serves 4.

SNOW PEAS AND MUSHROOMS

1 6-oz. pkg. frozen snow peas *or* 2 c. fresh
  snow peas
  Water to cover
1 t. salt
1 4-oz. can mushroom bits and pieces
2 T. melted butter

Cook frozen snow peas or fresh snow peas in salted water to cover for 20 minutes or until tender. Add drained mushrooms. Mix well. Heat through. Drain. Pour into warm serving dish. Pour melted butter over peas. Serve hot. Serves 4.

CAULIFLOWER WITH
BUTTERED CRUMBS

1 head cauliflower
1 t. salt
  Water to cover
3 T. margarine
¾ c. bread crumbs

Soak cauliflower in salted cold water, head down for 30 minutes. Rinse in clear water. Place in kettle. Add salt and enough water to cover. Simmer slowly for 20 to 30 minutes, until tender but still firm. Drain. Carefully remove cauliflower to a warm serving dish. Melt margarine in saucepan or small skillet and mix with bread crumbs. Heat through, but do not burn. Pour over cauliflower and serve hot. Serves 6.

STEWED TOMATOES WITH
BREAD CUBES

1 30-oz. can tomatoes *or* 2 c.
  fresh tomatoes
1 c. stale bread, cut in cubes
1 t. salt
1 T. butter
½ t. pepper

Heat tomatoes in a saucepan or cook fresh tomatoes 20 minutes. Add bread cubes, butter, and seasonings. Bring to a boil. Serve hot. Serves 4.

STEWED TOMATOES

1 30-oz. can tomatoes *or* 2 c. fresh
  tomatoes
1 t. salt
1 T. butter
½ t. pepper

Combine tomatoes, seasonings and butter in a saucepan. Bring to a boil. Serve hot. Serves 4.

PARSNIP PATTIES

8 to 10 parsnips
½ t. salt
  Boiling water
½ t. onion salt
⅛ t. pepper
½ t. salt
1 egg, beaten
⅓ c. fine bread crumbs
2 T. butter or margarine
¼ c. bread crumbs

Peel parsnips and cook in boiling salted water until tender. Drain and mash. Beat in seasonings and egg. Add bread crumbs. Chill well. Make into 6 patties. Coat with additional bread crumbs and fry in melted butter until golden brown on both sides. Serves 6.

Meats and Main Dishes

SAUERBRATEN

5 lbs. boneless round, chuck or
    rump roast
2 onions, sliced
2 carrots, pared and sliced
1 stalk celery, chopped
1 T. meat tenderizer
1 T. salt
2 T. sugar
6 peppercorns
3 bay leaves
6 whole cloves
1½ c. red wine vinegar
1½ c. water
2 T. flour
4 T. butter
½ c. gingersnap crumbs

Place meat in earthenware, glass or enamel bowl. Add vegetables, meat tenderizer, seasonings, vinegar and water. Cover and refrigerate for 2 to 4 days, turning meat each day. When ready to cook, remove meat from marinade and pat dry. Strain marinade and save both marinade and vegetables. Flour meat. In a deep pot, melt butter and brown meat on all sides. Add 2 cups marinade and the vegetables. Cover tightly and simmer over low heat for 3½ to 4 hours, or until meat is tender. Add a bit more marinade if needed to replenish liquid. Remove meat to a heated platter and keep warm. To make gravy, strain vegetables from marinade. Add enough of the marinade to make 2 cups. Bring to a boil; add gingersnap crumbs. Cook, stirring constantly until thickened. Serve with vegetables, gravy and potato dumplings. Serves 12.

Pictured opposite
Chicken-Broccoli Casserole
(page 27)

CHICKEN-BROCCOLI CASSEROLE

3 lb. frying chicken
2 10-oz. pkgs. frozen broccoli *or*
    2 bunches fresh broccoli
1 c. mayonnaise
2 10¾-oz. cans condensed cream of
    chicken soup
¼ t. curry powder
1 T. lemon juice
½ c. grated Cheddar cheese
½ c. bread crumbs
1 T. melted butter

Stew chicken; cool and bone. Steam broccoli until tender; drain. Grease an 11 x 7-inch casserole. Place chicken on the bottom, broccoli on top. Combine mayonnaise, soup, curry powder and lemon juice. Pour over broccoli. Sprinkle with a mixture of cheese and bread crumbs combined with butter. Bake in a 350° oven for 30 minutes. Serves 6.

BIG BOY PIE

½ c. chopped onion
¼ c. shortening
1 lb. ground beef
2 T. catsup or chili sauce
1 t. salt
2 c. biscuit mix
⅔ c. milk
1 c. cooked tomatoes, drained
1 c. grated cheese

Sauté onion in shortening until golden. Add meat and brown. Stir in catsup and salt. Set aside. Stir milk into the biscuit mix, stirring until well blended. Turn onto a lightly floured board. Knead six times. Roll into a circular shape and place in a 9-inch pie pan. Fill with meat and onion. Cover with tomatoes and top with grated cheese. Bake in a 450° oven for 30 minutes. Serves 6.

LASAGNA

1 lb. ground beef
¼ c. butter
1 c. chopped onion
1 garlic bud, minced
3 6-oz. cans tomato paste
2 c. water
2½ T. salt
1 No. 2 can tomatoes
1 lb. broad noodles, boiled
1 lb. mozzarella cheese, shredded
2 lbs. dry cottage cheese
1 c. Parmesan cheese

Brown meat in butter. Add onion and garlic. Stir in tomato paste, water, salt, and tomatoes. Cook over low heat for 45 minutes. Cook noodles, rinse and drain. Butter a 13 x 9 x 2-inch baking dish. Line dish with layer of noodles, sauce and cheese, ending with sauce and cheese. Bake in a 375° oven for 30 minutes. Let stand for 10 minutes before cutting. Serves 8 to 10.

VEAL PARMIGIANA

1½ lbs. veal, thinly sliced
3 T. vegetable oil
½ c. chopped onion
2 8-oz. cans tomato sauce
¼ t. crushed basil leaves
½ t. oregano
¼ t. thyme
½ lb. sliced mozzarella cheese
¼ c. grated Parmesan cheese

Over medium heat, brown veal lightly on both sides in the hot oil. Remove meat to a shallow 2-quart buttered dish. Add more oil as needed. Add onion and sauté until tender. Stir in tomato sauce, basil, oregano and thyme. Remove from heat. Pour sauce over veal and top with mozzarella and Parmesan cheese. Bake in a 350° oven for 40 minutes or until browned and tender. Serves 6.

CHOW MEIN CASSEROLE

1 lb. ground beef
1 onion, chopped
1 large can chow mein noodles
2 c. diced celery
2 T. vegetable oil
1 10¾-oz. can condensed cream of mushroom soup
1 10¾-oz. can condensed tomato soup
1 10¾-oz. can condensed cream of chicken soup

Brown beef and onion in oil. Pour into a greased 2-quart casserole. Add celery, noodles and soup. Bake in a 350° oven for 1 hour. Serves 6.

HAM LOAF

2½ c. soft bread crumbs
1 c. milk
1 lb. ground ham
1 lb. ground beef
2 eggs
½ green pepper, chopped
2 T. chopped onion
1 t. salt
½ t. pepper

Soak bread crumbs in milk. Add to meat and mix well. Add remaining ingredients and mix thoroughly. Pack in a greased loaf pan. Bake in a 350° oven for 1½ hours. Serves 6.

BAKED SPARERIBS AND DRESSING

1 c. chopped apple
1 c. hot water
4 c. dry bread crumbs
1 t. sage
½ c. chopped onion
1 t. salt
4 lbs. meaty pork spareribs

In a large bowl, combine all ingredients except spareribs. Add more water if a moist stuffing is desired. Place dressing in the bottom of a greased baking dish. Place ribs on top. Cover tightly with foil. Bake in a 350° oven for 2 hours or until meat is tender. Serves 4 to 6.

CORNED BEEF HASH

4 c. cooked corned beef, diced
2 T. butter
4 c. cooked potatoes, diced
1 medium onion, diced
1 t. salt
½ t. pepper
½ to 1 c. milk
6 poached eggs

Melt butter in a heavy frying pan; add chopped meat, potatoes, onion, seasonings and enough milk to moisten. Stir until well blended. Cook slowly for 1 hour. When brown on bottom, fold over like an omelet and serve on a warm platter. Garnish with poached eggs. Serves 6.

TAMALE PIE

1 onion, chopped
1 green pepper, diced
1 T. shortening
2 8-oz. cans tomato sauce
1 12-oz. can whole kernel corn
½ c. ripe olives, chopped
1 clove garlic, minced
1 T. sugar
1 t. salt
½ t. pepper
1 t. chili powder
1½ c. shredded American cheese
¾ lb. ground beef
¾ c. cornmeal
½ t. salt
2 c. cold water
1 T. butter

Cook onion and green pepper in shortening until tender. Add meat and brown. Add tomato sauce, corn, olives, garlic, sugar, salt, pepper and chili powder. Simmer for 20 to 25 minutes. Add cheese, stirring until melted. Pour into a 10 x 6-inch greased baking dish and set aside. Stir cornmeal and salt into water. Cook and stir until thick. Add butter. Spoon over meat mixture in strips. Bake in a 375° oven for about 40 minutes. Serves 6 to 8.

JAMBALAYA

½ lb. bacon
½ c. finely chopped onion
2 large green peppers, chopped
1 c. uncooked rice
1 clove garlic, minced
1 large can tomatoes
1 t. salt
1 bay leaf
¼ t. thyme
½ lb. baked or cooked ham, cubed
2 T. chopped parsley
½ t. pepper
½ t. Tabasco sauce
2 c. chicken broth, strained
1 lb. shrimp, cooked, shelled, and deveined

Preheat oven to 350°. Cut bacon into ½-inch pieces and cook in a heavy, oven-proof pan or Dutch oven with cover. When browned, remove with slotted spoon to paper towel to drain. Sauté onion until transparent, stirring as needed. Add green pepper; cook for 1 minute. Add rice; stir and cook rice for 3 minutes. Add remaining ingredients and bring to a boil. Cover pot and place in oven. Bake, covered, for 15 to 20 minutes or until liquid is absorbed and rice is tender. Sprinkle with parsley. Serves 4 to 6.

BEEF AND SAUERKRAUT

1 qt. sauerkraut
2 T. flour
3 lbs. beef brisket
1 small onion, minced
1 tart apple, grated
1 T. brown sugar
½ t. salt
¼ t. pepper

In a large Dutch oven, layer half of the sauerkraut; sprinkle with flour. Add meat, onion, apple and sugar. Sprinkle with salt and pepper. Lay remaining sauerkraut on top of meat. Add boiling water to just cover. Cover tightly and simmer for 1½ to 2 hours over low heat. Serves 6.

LAMB STEW WITH MUSHROOM DUMPLINGS

3 lbs. lamb stew meat, cubed
3 T. shortening
½ c. sliced onion
3 carrots, sliced diagonally
5 c. boiling water
1 c. flour
2 t. baking powder
½ c. condensed mushroom soup
3 T. water
3 T. parsley, chopped

Roll lamb in flour. Melt shortening and brown lamb cubes and onion. Add carrots and boiling water. Simmer slowly for 2 hours. To make dumplings, sift together flour and baking powder. Add mushroom soup and water. Mix well. After stew has simmered for 2 hours, drop dumplings by spoonfuls into boiling stew. Cover tightly and cook for 20 minutes. Remove stew to hot platter and surround with dumplings. Garnish with parsley. Serves 6.

BEEF STROGANOFF

3 beef bouillon cubes
1 c. boiling water
2 lbs. round or sirloin steak, cubed
3 T. flour
½ t. salt
⅛ t. pepper
½ c. shortening
1 c. chopped onion
1 14-oz. can mushrooms
1 c. sour cream
1 T. Worcestershire sauce

Dissolve bouillon cubes in water. Set aside. Dredge meat in flour and seasonings. In a large skillet, brown in ¼ cup of the shortening. Sauté onion in remaining shortening; add onion and bouillon to meat. Mix thoroughly. Cover pan and cook slowly for 1½ hours or until meat is tender. Add mushrooms and Worcestershire sauce; fold in sour cream. Heat thoroughly but do not boil. Serve hot on buttered noodles. Serves 6.

LAMB STEW

2 lbs. lamb shoulder, cubed
1 t. salt
4 carrots, cut up
3 potatoes, quartered
1 t. sugar
2 T. flour
1 T. shortening
1 6-oz. can peas

Salt meat thoroughly and place in a stewing pan; add water to cover. Bring to a boil. Reduce heat and simmer until meat is almost tender. Add carrots, potatoes and sugar. Simmer until vegetables and meat are tender. Melt shortening; stir in flour. Add about a cup of hot stew liquid to flour mixture, stirring well. Add to stew, stirring until thickened. Add drained peas. Heat through. Serves 4 to 6.

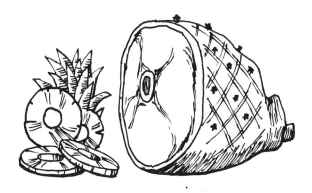

BAKED HAM

5 to 6-lb. ham
½ c. whole cloves
⅓ c. prepared mustard
½ c. brown sugar
6 to 8 pineapple slices
½ c. pineapple juice

Bake ham in roasting pan, uncovered, in a 350° oven for 1½ hours. Remove from oven and cut off skin. With a sharp knife, score fat into diamond shapes. Place a whole clove in the center of each diamond. Spread mustard over ham. Then press on brown sugar. Secure pineapple slices on ham with toothpicks. Bake an additional 30 minutes, basting frequently with pineapple juice. Serves 10 to 12.

Pictured opposite
Beef Stroganoff
(page 31)

NOODLE, KRAUT AND WIENER CASSEROLE

6 wieners
1 c. sauerkraut, rinsed and drained
½ t. caraway seed
⅛ t. celery salt
1 c. cooked noodles
½ t. pepper
½ t. salt
½ t. nutmeg
4 oz. Cheddar cheese, shredded
1 T. margarine

Place wieners in a buttered 1½-quart casserole. Combine sauerkraut, caraway seed and celery salt. Combine noodles, pepper, salt, and nutmeg. Mix well. Place half of the sauerkraut on top of wieners. Cover with noodles. Arrange cheese and margarine over noodles. Top with rest of the sauerkraut. Bake in a 375° oven for 25 minutes. Makes 2 servings.

CHOP SUEY

1 c. pork or veal, cubed
½ c. chopped onion
3 T. shortening
1½ c. water
½ t. salt
1½ c. celery, cut diagonally
1 1-lb. can bean sprouts
1 1-lb. can chop suey vegetables, drained
1 4-oz. can mushrooms
3 T. cornstarch
⅓ c. cold water
1 T. brown sugar
2 T. soy sauce
2 c. cooked rice

Brown cubed meat and onion in shortening. Place in stewing kettle. Add water, salt and celery; simmer until meat is tender. Add bean sprouts, chop suey vegetables, and mushrooms. Heat to boiling. Mix cornstarch and cold water until smooth. Add to boiling mixture, stirring constantly, until thickened and transparent. Add brown sugar and soy sauce. Serve over cooked rice or Chinese noodles. Serves 4.

SAN FRANCISCO STEW

1½ lbs. hamburger
2 T. shortening
1 1-lb. can tomatoes
4 c. Great Northern beans, cooked
1 large onion, sliced
1 c. brown sugar, firmly packed
4 bacon slices

Brown meat in shortening. Drain beans; add to meat with tomatoes. Mash. Pour half the mixture in a 4-quart greased baking dish. Slice a layer of onion to cover; sprinkle brown sugar over onions. Add remaining bean mixture. Bake in a 350° oven for 1 hour. Place bacon slices over top. Bake until bacon is done and juice is absorbed. Serves 6.

PARSNIP CASSEROLE

3 c. mashed, cooked parsnips
½ t. pepper
½ t. salt
1 c. cubed ham
1 c. sliced mushrooms
1 c. shredded cheese
½ c. crushed cornflakes

Season hot parsnips. Mix ham, mushrooms and cheese. Alternate layers of parsnips and ham mixture in a greased 2-quart casserole. Sprinkle top with cornflakes. Bake in a 350° oven for 25 minutes. Serves 6.

MACARONI CASSEROLE

1 lb. ground beef
2 t. dry onion flakes
2 c. elbow macaroni
1 T. diced pimiento
1 3-oz. can tomato sauce
⅔ c. water
2 T. vegetable oil

Brown ground beef in oil. Add onion flakes. Cook macaroni in salted water until done. Drain and rinse with hot water. Combine macaroni and meat. Add tomato sauce, water and pimiento. Pour into a greased baking dish. Cover with foil. Bake for 1 hour in a 350° oven. Serves 6.

ORIENTAL HAMBURGER

1½ lbs. ground beef
2 T. shortening
1 medium onion, chopped
2 t. garlic salt
2 c. water
4 T. soy sauce
1½ T. molasses
1 8-oz. pkg. frozen green beans
4 T. cornstarch
½ c. water
6 to 7 c. cooked rice

Brown ground beef and onion in shortening. Stir in garlic salt, 2 cups water, soy sauce and molasses. Heat to boiling; add green beans. Simmer 20 to 30 minutes until beans are tender. Blend cornstarch with ½ cup water. Stir into meat mixture; cook until thickens. Serve over rice. Serves 4 to 6.

HUNTER'S STEW

2 lbs. lean meat, beef or venison, cubed
Shank bone of beef
½ lb. suet
1½ gal. cold water or 24 c.
1 bunch celery
3 onions, chopped
1½ c. peas
1½ c. corn
1½ c. tomatoes
1½ c. lima beans
5 potatoes, diced
1½ c. diced carrot
¼ c. rice
½ c. chili sauce

Combine meat, bone, suet, celery, onion and water. Simmer 2½ hours. Remove celery and bone. Add vegetables with rice and simmer over low heat until vegetables are done. Before serving, season with ½ cup chili sauce and more salt and pepper if needed. Should be a thick soup. Serves 8 to 10.

SAVORY STEW

2 lbs. beef chuck, cut in 1-inch cubes
1 t. lemon juice
1 clove garlic, minced
1 small bay leaf
¼ t. allspice
8 small whole onions
3 c. water
1 t. Worcestershire sauce
1 medium onion, sliced
2 t. salt
¼ t. pepper
6 carrots, quartered
3 medium potatoes, cut up
½ c. flour
1 c. water

In Dutch oven, combine all ingredients except 1 cup of the water and the flour. Cover and bake in a 325° oven for 4 hours or until meat is tender. Remove stew from oven. In a covered jar, shake 1 cup water and flour until blended. Stir into stew. Heat to boiling, stirring constantly for 1 minute. Serve hot. Serves 4 to 6.

PRIME RIBS AU JUS

5 lbs. prime ribs
1 c. water
¼ c. vinegar
2 stalks celery, diced
1 c. water
⅛ c. vegetable oil
2 carrots, diced
1 onion, chopped
2 bay leaves
½ t. sage
½ t. salt
4 raw potatoes, cut up
1 green pepper, diced
1 clove garlic
½ t. thyme
2 c. tomatoes
¼ t. pepper
1 t. paprika

Place beef in roasting pan with water. Add ingredients in order as above. Bake in a 300° oven for 2½ hours. Baste meat every 30 minutes. Serves 6.

SOY-MARINATED CHUCK STEAK

3½ to 4 lbs. beef blade chuck roast,
    2 inches thick
    Unseasoned meat tenderizer
3 T. brown sugar
4 t. white vinegar
¾ c. soy sauce
3 T. Worcestershire sauce

Early in the day, trim excess fat from steak. Prepare steak with meat tenderizer as label directs. Combine brown sugar, vinegar, soy sauce and Worcestershire sauce in a deep bowl or pan. Add meat, turning to coat. Cover and refrigerate at least 4 hours, turning occasionally. Barbecue, basting with marinade, until tender and browned. Serves 4 to 6.

SWEET-SOUR RIBS

3 lbs. beef short ribs
1 c. sliced onion
1 clove garlic
1 small bay leaf
3 T. brown sugar
¼ c. raisins
⅛ t. pepper
1½ c. hot water
¼ c. vinegar
⅓ c. catsup
1 t. salt

Wipe short ribs with damp cloth. Cut into individual serving pieces. Remove excess fat. Dredge in seasoned flour and brown well on all sides in hot fat in skillet. Remove ribs. Sauté onion and garlic. Combine remaining ingredients; pour over ribs. Cover and simmer 2 to 2½ hours or over low heat until tender. Serves 6.

BAKED HAM HASH

½ lb. boiled ham, ground
1 6-oz. can peas
5 hard-boiled eggs, chopped
1½ c. soft bread crumbs
1 T. melted butter
1 c. milk
2 T. flour
⅛ t. pepper
½ t. salt

In a buttered casserole, layer ham, peas, eggs and bread crumbs. Melt butter in a saucepan. Stir in flour. Gradually add milk, stirring constantly. Cook over medium heat, stirring constantly, until thickened. Add salt and pepper. Pour over casserole. Serves 4 to 6.

PIGSPAGOOT

2 T. shortening
2 lbs. pork, cubed
1 stalk celery, chopped
1 27-oz. can tomatoes
1 9-oz. pkg. spaghetti, cooked
1 6-oz. can mushrooms, drained
1 8-oz. can lima beans
1 3-oz. jar stuffed olives and liquid

Slightly brown pork in shortening. Salt very lightly. Sauté celery in 1 tablespoon shortening. Add to browned pork. Mix in tomatoes. Simmer until meat is tender. Add cooked spaghetti, mushrooms, lima beans, olives and liquid. Heat through; serve hot. Serves 4 to 6.

HORSERADISH MOLD
FOR COLD MEAT

1 3-oz. pkg. lime gelatin
1 c. boiling water
1 c. cold water
¾ c. grated horseradish
1 c. shredded cabbage

Dissolve gelatin in boiling water; add cold water. Stir in horseradish and cabbage. Pour into tiny individual molds and chill until firm. Serve in lettuce nests as a garnish for a platter of cold meat.

Pictured opposite
Sweet-Sour Ribs
(page 34)

NEW ENGLAND BOILED DINNER

2 lbs. ham hocks
6 small beets
3 small turnips
3 carrots
1 t. salt
6 small onions
2 c. shredded cabbage
3 small parsnips
3 small potatoes
½ t. pepper

Wash ham hocks and put in a stewing kettle with enough water to cover. Simmer for 1 hour. Add vegetables in serving sized portions and seasonings. Cover and cook 30 minutes more or until vegetables and meat are tender. Place ham hocks in middle of platter and arrange vegetables around edge. Serves 4 to 6.

STUFFED FLANK STEAK

2 lbs. flank steak
1½ t. salt
1 onion, chopped
2 apples, sliced
6 or 8 prunes
Strips of fat salt pork
2 T. shortening
3 T. flour
½ t. pepper
1 c. cream
Toothpicks

Pound meat; salt. Sprinkle evenly with onions, apples, and prunes and roll tightly. Tie or fasten with toothpicks. Insert strips of pork. Sear on all sides in hot shortening. Cover and simmer, basting with the stock. Cook for 2 hours. Remove meat; add flour to liquid in pan. Add cream and pepper. Simmer until thick. Pour over meat. Serves 4 to 6.

LIVER LOAF

1 lb. ground liver
¼ lb. ground pork
¼ lb. ground beef
2 t. salt
¼ t. nutmeg
4 T. chopped onion
2 T. shortening
2 eggs
2 c. thin cream
¼ t. cinnamon
1 t. pepper
2 c. flour, sifted

Combine all meats, salt and nutmeg; mix well. Sauté onion in shortening until tender. Add to ground meat with eggs. Blend in remaining ingredients. Put mixture in a well-greased loaf pan. Set in a pan with hot water 1-inch deep. Cover loaf pan with foil. Bake in a 350° oven for 1 hour. Uncover and bake 1 additional hour. Serve hot or cold. Serves 8 to 10.

CREAMED CHIPPED BEEF

¼ lb. dried beef
2 T. minced onion
1 4-oz. can mushrooms
¼ c. butter
3 T. flour
1 c. milk
1 c. shredded Cheddar cheese
1 t. salt
⅛ t. pepper
1 c. sour cream

Cut dried beef in strips. Sauté beef, onion and drained mushrooms in butter. Cook over low heat until onions are transparent. Blend in flour. Add milk, stirring constantly. Cook until sauce is thick and smooth. Add cheese, sour cream, salt and pepper. Heat to serving temperature. Serve in popovers, on buttered toast triangles, toasted English muffins, rice or buttered noodles. Garnish with additional cheese, if desired. Serves 5 to 6.

SPANISH RICE

1 lb. ground beef
2 T. vegetable oil
1 green pepper, chopped
1 onion, chopped
1 1-lb. can tomatoes
3 T. parsley
1 c. diced celery
1 c. raw rice
1 c. water
½ t. salt
¼ t. pepper
½ t. chili pepper

Brown ground beef in oil. Add pepper and onion and cook until onion is transparent. Add remaining ingredients, mixing well. Pour mixture into a greased 1½-quart casserole. Bake in a 350° oven for 45 minutes. Serves 4.

SATURDAY NOODLE BAKE

1 lb. ground beef
½ lb. ground pork
2 T. butter or margarine
⅔ c. chopped onion
2 10¾-oz. cans condensed tomato soup
1 3-oz. pkg. cream cheese
2 T. sugar
¼ t. pepper
1 t. salt
1½ T. Worcestershire sauce
2 c. wide noodles
1 c. crushed cornflakes
½ c. melted butter or margarine

Combine meats and brown lightly in butter. Add onion and cook until tender, but not brown. Add soup, cheese, sugar, Worcestershire sauce and seasonings. Simmer for 15 minutes. Cook noodles in boiling water until tender; drain. Place noodles in a 11 x 7 x 1-inch buttered baking dish; pour sauce over noodles. Mix cornflakes with melted butter; sprinkle over the top. Bake in a 350° oven for 20 minutes or until heated through. Serves 8.

PORK ROAST

4 to 5-lb. fresh pork shoulder
½ t. pepper
1 t. salt
¼ c. flour
6 potatoes, quartered
6 medium onions, quartered
6 carrots, halved

Place pork shoulder, fat side up, in a roasting pan. Sprinkle with salt and pepper. Sprinkle flour on fat part of roast. Roast in a 350° oven for 1½ hours. Prepare vegetables and place around meat. Bake an additional 45 minutes or until vegetables are tender and pork is well done. Serves 6 to 8.

PORK, SAUERKRAUT AND DUMPLINGS

3 or 4 pork shanks *or* 3 lbs. meaty spareribs
1 large onion, chopped
1 T. caraway seed
1 t. salt
½ t. pepper
1½ lbs. sauerkraut

Wash pork. Place in a large pot; cover with water. Bring to a boil and simmer for about 15 minutes. Add onion, caraway seed, salt and pepper. Simmer for 60 minutes. Rinse sauerkraut; add to the meat. Bring to a boil and add dumplings. Cover tightly and boil an additional 30 minutes.

POTATO DUMPLINGS

1 egg, slightly beaten
½ c. flour
4 large potatoes, peeled and grated
½ t. salt

Drain excess water from grated potatoes by placing on cloth and squeezing out excess water. Place potatoes in a bowl and add egg, salt and flour; mix thoroughly. Drop by spoonfuls on top of pork and sauerkraut mixture. Simmer about 30 minutes. Serves 4 to 6.

STEAK AND KIDNEY PIE

1 lb. round steak
1 beef kidney
¼ c. flour
⅛ t. pepper
1 t. salt
3 T. shortening
1 onion, chopped
¼ c. pimiento, chopped
2 T. Worcestershire sauce
¼ t. thyme
1½ c. water
Pastry for 1 pie

Cut round steak in ¾ to 1-inch cubes. Remove tubes and fat from kidney. Cut in ¾ to 1-inch cubes. Combine flour, salt and pepper. Dredge steak and kidney cubes in flour, reserving any extra flour. Brown meat in shortening. Remove meat from skillet. Add onion to drippings in skillet and sauté over low heat until transparent. Drain grease. Add pimiento, Worcestershire sauce, thyme and water. Bring to a boil. Stir in browned meat cubes and any remaining seasoned flour. Make crust for pie. Roll out and line pie pan. Roll out top crust, cutting design for steam to escape. Turn meat mixture into crust in pie pan. Moisten edges. Cover with top crust. Seal top crust to edge and flute edges. Paint top with milk. Bake in a 325° oven for 1½ hrs. Makes 6 servings.

SAUERKRAUT CASSEROLE

2 lbs. sauerkraut
½ c. diced smoked sausage
1 large carrot, diced
1 onion, chopped
12 peppercorns
1 c. dry white wine
2 c. diced smoked ham
½ c. diced bacon
1 large apple, diced
1 large potato, pared and grated
1 c. stock or water

Drain sauerkraut. Combine all ingredients and pour in a buttered 2-quart casserole. Cover tightly and bake in a 350° oven for 1½ to 2 hours. It should be fairly dry. Serves 6.

TUNA-POTATO CHIP CASSEROLE

2 c. tuna, flaked
2 T. butter
1 c. sliced fresh mushrooms
½ green pepper, diced
1 t. minced onion
½ c. sliced stuffed olives
1 3-oz. bag potato chips
2 c. White Sauce

Melt butter in skillet. Sauté mushrooms, pepper and onion over low heat for 5 minutes. In a greased casserole, lightly combine all ingredients. Top with crushed potato chips. Bake in a 375° oven for 30 minutes. Serves 4.

WHITE SAUCE

2 T. butter
2 T. flour
2 c. milk

Melt butter; stir in flour. Slowly add milk, blending until smooth. Cook slowly until thickened, stirring constantly.

HUNGARIAN VEAL CUTLET

1 veal steak, 1½-inch thick
1 c. soft bread crumbs
1 egg, slightly beaten
1 T. water
1 clove garlic
¼ c. shortening
1 t. paprika
2 c. sour cream

Cut veal into six serving-size pieces. Dip into crumbs, in egg that has been beaten with water, and again into crumbs. Rub frying pan with garlic; melt shortening. Brown breaded veal quickly on both sides. Add paprika to sour cream. Pour over veal. Cover; and bake in a 325° oven for 1½ hours or until tender. Uncover for the last 15 minutes to brown. Serves 6.

*Pictured opposite
Ingredients for
Sauerkraut Casserole
(page 38)*

PORK CHOPS SPANISH STYLE

6 pork chops *or* pork steaks
  Pepper
  Salt
2 T. shortening
2 16-oz. cans stewed tomatoes
1 c. uncooked rice
2 T. butter
1 t. salt

Sprinkle meat with salt and pepper. Brown meat in hot shortening. Drain. Preheat oven to 350°. In a 1½-quart greased baking dish, combine tomatoes with liquid, rice, butter and 1 teaspoon salt. Arrange meat over rice. Bake for 1 hour or until meat is tender. Serves 4.

MEATBALLS WITH SAUERKRAUT

1 lb. ground beef
1 egg
¼ c. coarse bread crumbs
½ t. salt
¼ t. pepper
1 c. catsup
1 c. water
½ c. gingersnap crumbs
¼ c. brown sugar, firmly packed
½ t. salt
1 8-oz. can sauerkraut

Mix together meat, egg, bread crumbs, salt and pepper. Shape into 1-inch balls. Simmer catsup, water and cookie crumbs for 5 minutes. Add brown sugar, salt and sauerkraut. Heat to boiling; add meatballs. Lower heat and simmer for 45 minutes. Serves 4 to 6.

ENGLISH BEEF STEW

1½ lbs. round steak, cubed
⅛ t. pepper
½ t. salt
3 T. shortening
2 medium onions, sliced
2 c. boiling water
2 c. tomatoes
3 c. sliced potatoes
1 T. Worcestershire sauce
1 c. sliced carrots
3 T. flour
¼ c. water
  Pastry or biscuits for topping

Season meat with salt and pepper and roll in flour. Brown in shortening. Add onions and boiling water. Simmer for ½ hour. Add tomatoes, potatoes, Worcestershire sauce and carrots. Simmer over low heat until meat and vegetables are tender. Remove meat and vegetables to a casserole and thicken stock with flour mixed with water. Pour thickened stock over meat and vegetables. Cover with biscuits. Bake in a 425° oven for 20 to 25 minutes. Serve hot. Serves 6.

FRANKY NOODLE

1 lb. frankfurters
1 onion, chopped
½ green pepper, chopped
3 T. margarine
1½ c. tomato juice
¾ c. water
1 T. sugar
2 T. flour
3 c. cooked noodles

Cut frankfurters into 1-inch pieces. Sauté franks, onion and green pepper in margarine. Add tomato juice, water, flour and sugar. Stir until thickened. Simmer slowly for 20 minutes; serve hot over noodles. Serve with salad and rolls. Serves 4.

PORK BIRDS

1 onion, chopped
½ c. chopped celery
1 T. shortening
1 t. sage
2 c. dry bread cubes
2 bouillon cubes
½ to ¾ c. hot water or enough to moisten bread
6 boneless pork steaks
2 T. shortening

Brown onion and celery in shortening. Add sage, onion and celery to bread cubes. Dissolve bouillon cubes in hot water and pour over bread mixture. Stir with a fork until moistened. Place a heaping tablespoon of stuffing in middle of pork steak. Roll up and fasten with toothpicks. Brown each steak in additional shortening until all sides are browned. Place in a casserole or baking dish; add ¾ cup water to bottom of pan. Cover and bake in a 350° oven 1½ hours. Serves 6.

FRANKFURTER SPAGHETTI

⅓ c. chopped onion
¼ c. shortening
3 T. flour
¼ t. oregano
½ t. salt
¼ t. pepper
¾ c. water
1 c. evaporated milk
1 t. Worcestershire sauce
1 c. grated American cheese
1 lb. wieners, cut up
1½ c. cooked spaghetti

Sauté onion in shortening until tender. Remove from heat and stir in flour, oregano, salt and pepper. Heat until thick; gradually add water, milk, Worcestershire sauce and cheese. Stir over low heat until cheese melts. Add wieners and spaghetti. Place in 1½-quart greased baking dish. Bake in a 350° oven for 30 minutes. Serves 4 to 6.

QUICK CHILI MAC

1 c. macaroni
1 green pepper, chopped
1 large onion, chopped
2 T. margarine
1 lb. ground beef
1 10¾-oz. can condensed tomato soup
1 1-lb. can kidney beans
½ t. salt
½ t. chili powder

Boil macaroni as directed on package. Drain and set aside. Sauté green pepper and onion in margarine until transparent. Add ground beef and brown. Add tomato soup, kidney beans, salt and chili powder. Simmer over low heat for 20 minutes. Add macaroni and heat through. Serves 4.

THRIFTY TUNA CASSEROLE

1 10¾-oz. can condensed cream of mushroom soup
½ c. milk
1 7-oz. can tuna, drained and flaked
1¾ c. potato chips, crushed
1 c. canned peas, drained

Empty soup into small bowl. Add milk and mix. Add tuna, crushed potato chips and peas. Stir well. Turn into a greased 1½-quart casserole. Sprinkle top with crushed potato chips. Bake in a 375° oven for 25 minutes. Serves 4.

VEAL SCALLOPINI

1 c. mushrooms
¼ c. olive oil or vegetable oil
¾ c. flour
2 lbs. veal steak, cut thin
½ t. pepper
1 t. salt
1½ c. white wine

Sauté mushrooms in hot oil. Remove and set aside. Flour meat lightly; brown in hot oil. Add mushrooms, salt, pepper and wine. Cover and simmer 20 minutes. Serves 6.

Quick Breads and Yeast Breads

CRANBERRY NUT LOAF

2 c. flour
1½ t. baking powder
1 t. salt
½ t. baking soda
1 egg
1 c. sugar
¾ c. orange juice
3 T. vegetable oil
1½ c. cranberries, chopped
1 c. chopped nuts

Sift together flour, baking powder, salt and soda. Put egg, sugar, orange juice and oil in blender. Blend only until mixed. Add cranberries and nuts; blend. Add dry ingredients and stir until barely moistened. Turn into a greased 9 x 5 x 3-inch loaf pan. Bake in a 350° oven for 45 minutes or until a tester inserted into the middle comes out clean. Turn out of pan onto a wire rack and cool before slicing.

BANANA BREAD

1 c. sugar
½ c. butter or margarine
1 t. baking soda
1 T. sour milk or orange juice
2 eggs, well beaten
3 mashed, ripe bananas
2 c. flour
¼ c. chopped nuts

Cream together butter and sugar. Stir soda into sour milk or orange juice. Add eggs, bananas, soda mixture and flour, beating thoroughly. Stir in nuts. Pour into a buttered loaf pan. Bake in a 350° oven for 1 hour. Cool before slicing. Freezes well. Makes 1 loaf.

CLUSTER COFFEE CAKE

2 pkgs. dry yeast
¼ c. warm water
1¼ c. milk, scalded and cooled to lukewarm
3½ to 4 c. flour
2 eggs, well beaten
½ c. sugar
½ c. melted butter and margarine
1 t. salt
2 T. grated orange rind
¾ c. sugar
¾ c. pecans, finely chopped

Soften yeast in water for 5 minutes. Add milk and 1 cup of the flour, beating well. Let mixture stand for 20 minutes or until light and bubbly. Blend beaten eggs, ½ cup sugar, melted butter and salt. Add to yeast mixture; mix well. Work in remaining flour and 1 tablespoon orange rind. Knead on floured board until dough is smooth and elastic. Place in a greased bowl and let rise in a warm place, until doubled in bulk. Divide dough in half; form each half into a long roll. Cut each roll into 24 pieces. Roll each piece into a ball. Mix remaining sugar and orange rind. Dip balls into melted butter, then into sugar mixed with rind, then into chopped nuts. Place in a greased tube pan, close together and in layers. Let stand in a warm place for 40 minutes. Bake in a 350° oven for 45 minutes. Turn out of pan onto a cake rack to cool. Break off pieces and butter. The coffee cake may be made in layer cake pans, if desired.

Pictured opposite
Cranberry Nut Loaf (upper shelf)
Banana Bread (lower shelf)
(page 43)

43

REFRIGERATOR ROLLS

1 c. milk, scalded
¼ c. sugar
1 t. salt
⅓ c. shortening *or* vegetable oil
2 pkgs. dry yeast
½ c. lukewarm water
2 eggs, beaten
5 c. sifted flour (about)

Scald milk. Add sugar, salt, shortening or oil. Stir until dissolved. Cool to lukewarm. Dissolve yeast in lukewarm water; add to milk mixture. Add eggs. Gradually add flour; mix to a smooth, soft dough. Knead on a lightly floured board until smooth and satiny. Shape into a ball and place in a greased bowl; cover with a cloth. Let rise in a warm place until doubled in bulk. (If it is not to be used immediately, dough can be set in refrigerator until needed; then let it rise until doubled in bulk.) Shape into rounds or crescents. Cover. Let rise until doubled in bulk. Bake in a 425° oven for 15 to 20 minutes. Makes 2½ dozen.

POPOVERS

1 c. flour
¼ t. salt
⅞ c. milk
1 t. melted butter or margarine
2 eggs

Sift together flour and salt. Gradually add milk to flour in a bowl. Add butter. Beat eggs well and add to batter. Beat batter for 2 minutes with mixer. Fill hot muffin pans two thirds full. Bake in a 450° oven for 14 minutes. Reduce heat to 350° and bake 20 more minutes. Serve hot. Can be filled with creamed vegetables or creamed meat.

PUMPKIN BREAD

1 c. brown sugar
½ c. sugar
1 c. cooked or canned pumpkin
½ c. vegetable oil
2 eggs, beaten
2 c. sifted flour
1 t. baking soda
½ t. salt
½ t. nutmeg
½ t. cinnamon
¼ t. ginger
1 c. raisins
½ c. chopped nuts
¼ c. water

Combine sugars, pumpkin, oil and eggs. Beat until blended. Sift together flour, soda, salt and spices. Add to pumpkin mixture and mix well. Stir in raisins, nuts and water. Spoon into a well-oiled 9 x 5 x 3-inch loaf pan. Bake in a 350° oven for 65 to 75 minutes or until a toothpick inserted into the bread comes out clean. Turn out on a wire rack to cool thoroughly before slicing.

BAKING POWDER BISCUITS

2 c. flour
1 t. salt
2 T. sugar
4 t. baking powder
2 T. shortening
½ c. milk, or enough to make a stiff dough

Sift flour, salt, sugar and baking powder into a bowl. Cut in shortening. Add milk, a little at a time, to make a stiff dough. Turn out on a floured board. Sprinkle flour over the top if sticky and pat into a circle about 1 inch thick. Cut into rounds with a biscuit cutter dipped in flour. Place in a greased pan; bake in a 400° oven for 15 to 20 minutes. Serve hot with butter and honey. *Note:* For shortcake, bake recipe in a 9-inch pie tin and split into wedges. Top with crushed berries and whipped cream.

BOSTON BROWN BREAD

1 egg
1 t. salt
2 T. sugar
1 T. shortening
1 c. sour milk
1 t. baking soda
2 T. dark molasses
2 T. white flour
1 c. raisins
1½ to 2 c. graham flour

Mix ingredients in order given. Care must be given that not too much graham flour is used as it makes the bread crumble when sliced. The dough should be a little thicker than cake batter. Bake in a greased loaf pan in a 350° oven for 50 to 60 minutes. Turn on wire rack to cool before slicing. Makes 1 loaf.

BRAN MUFFINS

1 c. whole bran
1 c. sour milk
1 c. flour
1 t. baking powder
½ t. salt
½ t. baking soda
½ t. cinnamon
¼ c. sugar
2 T. shortening
1 egg, well beaten

Pour milk over bran and set aside. Sift together flour, baking powder, salt, soda, cinnamon and sugar. Set aside. In a large bowl, beat shortening and egg; add bran mixture, mixing thoroughly. Add dry ingredients, stirring only until moistened. Fill muffin cups two-thirds full. Bake in a 400° oven for 20 to 25 minutes.

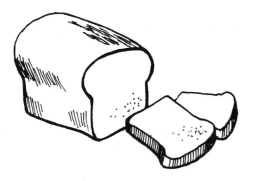

CHEESE BLINTZES

2 eggs
½ t. salt
1 c. water
1 c. sifted flour
¾ lb. cottage cheese
2 T. melted butter
2 T. light cream
⅛ t. salt
Butter for frying

Put 1 egg, salt, water and flour in blender container. Cover and process at mix until smooth. Pour 2 tablespoons of the batter onto a hot griddle. Fry on one side only until lightly browned, using low heat. Remove each pancake onto a clean cloth, cooked side up. Cool. Stir ¾ of the cottage cheese and remaining egg and butter together. Spread a little on each pancake. Fold over from both sides, then roll loosely. Sauté in hot butter. Put the cream, remaining cottage cheese and salt into blender container. Process at blend until smooth. Spoon onto hot blintzes and serve at once. Makes 4 servings.

CREAM PUFFS

¾ c. water
⅓ c. butter or margarine
¾ c. flour
⅛ t. salt
3 eggs

In a small saucepan combine water and butter and bring to a boil over medium heat. Remove from heat and beat in flour and salt, all at once. Over low heat, stir until mixture forms a ball and leaves the sides of the pan. Remove from heat. Add eggs all at once. Beat until smooth and satiny looking. Place dough by large spoonfuls on an ungreased cookie sheet. Bake in a 400° oven for 40 minutes without opening door. Remove from oven and cool in a draft-free place. To serve, cut tops from puffs and take out doughy substance in the middle of each puff and discard. Fill puff with cold vanilla pudding or ice cream. Place tops back on. Can be frosted with chocolate frosting.

DOUGHNUT DROPS

2 c. sifted flour
⅓ c. sugar
3 t. baking powder
½ t. salt
1 t. nutmeg
1 egg, slightly beaten
¾ c. milk
3 T. vegetable oil
Oil for frying
Confectioners' sugar or cinnamon and sugar mixture

Sift together dry ingredients. Add egg, milk and oil; stir until smooth. Heat 1 inch oil to 365°. Drop dough by teaspoons into hot oil. Turn after a few seconds and fry until browned on both sides, turning once more. Remove with slotted spoon. Drain on paper towels over a pan. Roll in sugar and serve warm. Makes about 3 dozen.

RAISED DOUGHNUTS

½ c. warm water
2 pkgs. dry yeast
½ c. shortening
1½ c. warm milk
½ c. sugar
2 eggs
6 to 6½ c. flour

Dissolve yeast in warm water. Heat shortening, milk and sugar until shortening melts. Remove from heat. Cool slightly; then stir in eggs. Stir in yeast mixture. Add 4 cups flour, mixing well. Add more flour as needed to make a soft dough. Knead until smooth and satiny. Place in a greased bowl and let rise in a warm place for 1 hour and 15 minutes. Punch down. Let rise 55 more minutes. Roll out on floured board to about a ¼-inch thickness. Cut with a doughnut cutter. Let rise for 30 minutes. Deep fry in hot grease at 400° until light brown. Turn to brown other side. Drain on paper towels. Sprinkle with confectioners' sugar, granulated sugar or frost.

POTATO BREAD

3 or 4 large potatoes
2 pkgs. dry yeast
¼ c. warm water
½ c. sugar
2 T. salt
½ c. melted shortening
4 c. scalded milk, cooled
4 to 6 c. flour or more

Dissolve yeast in warm water. Peel and cook potatoes. Drain and save potato water. Mash potatoes until fluffy. Add potato water, sugar, salt, yeast, shortening and milk. Add enough flour to make a thick sponge. Let set overnight in a warm place. In the morning, add enough flour to make a dough that isn't sticky. Make into loaves, biscuits or rolls. Let rise about 1 hour. Bake in a 350° oven 30 minutes for rolls and biscuits, about 1 hour for loaves. Remove from pans and wipe tops with butter, then cover with cloth to soften crust.

POTATO PANCAKES

2 eggs
½ small onion
½ t. salt
⅛ t. pepper
2 T. flour
¼ t. baking powder
3 c. cubed raw potatoes

Put eggs, onion, salt, pepper, flour, baking powder and ½ cup of the potato cubes into blender container. Process at grate until potatoes have gone through the blades. Stop blender and add remaining potatoes. Cover and process at chop just until all potato cubes have passed through the blades. Use a rubber spatula to help guide potatoes into the blades. Do not overblend. Pour onto a hot, well-greased griddle. Cook until golden brown. Drain on absorbent paper. Yield 12 pancakes. Serve hot with applesauce.

Note: Potatoes can be raw grated to make 1 cup. Drain well and use in above recipe.

Cakes and Frostings

BRANDIED FRUIT CAKE

3 c. sifted flour
1 t. salt
1 t. baking soda
1 t. nutmeg
1 t. cinnamon
¾ c. shortening
½ c. honey
½ c. brown sugar, firmly packed
2 eggs
½ c. brandy
1 lb. mixed candied fruit, diced
1 c. whole glacé cherries
1 c. light raisins
1 c. broken walnuts

Sift flour with salt, soda, nutmeg and cinnamon. Cream shortening, honey and sugar until fluffy. Add eggs, one at a time, beating well after each. Stir in brandy, fruits and nuts. Gradually add dry ingredients. Beat well with a spoon until well blended. Spoon into a greased and floured 9-inch tube pan. Bake in a 300° oven for 2½ hours or until a toothpick inserted in center comes out clean. Cool in pan for 15 minutes. Remove to rack to finish cooling. Wrap in foil and store to ripen. Once a week, open foil and sprinkle thoroughly with more brandy. Just before serving, brush with glaze and decorate with candied fruits.

COFFEE CLOUD SPONGE CAKE

1 T. instant coffee
1 c. boiling water
2 c. flour
3 t. baking powder
½ t. salt
6 eggs, separated
½ t. cream of tartar
2 c. sugar
1 t. vanilla
1 c. pecans, chopped

Dissolve instant coffee in boiling water. Set aside to cool. Sift together flour, baking powder and salt. Beat egg whites with cream of tartar. Add ½ cup of the sugar. Set aside. Beat egg yolks until blended. Add sugar and vanilla. Beat 4 to 5 minutes. Add dry ingredients, cooled coffee and egg whites. Fold in pecans. Bake in a greased and floured 10-inch tube pan or a 13 x 9 x 2-inch pan. Bake in a 350° oven for 60 to 70 minutes.

COFFEE ICING

2 T. butter, softened
2 c. confectioners' sugar
1½ t. instant coffee
2 T. milk

Mix the ingredients to a spreading consistency and spread on cake.

FRUIT CAKE GLAZE

2 T. brown sugar
1 T. light corn syrup
2 T. water

Combine ingredients in a saucepan. Bring to a boil and boil for 2 minutes. Cool before using.

SALAD DRESSING CAKE

2½ c. flour
1¼ c. sugar
⅓ c. cocoa
1½ t. baking soda
½ t. salt
¾ c. salad dressing
1 c. cold water
1 t. vanilla

Sift together flour, sugar, cocoa, soda and salt. Stir in salad dressing, cold water and vanilla, mixing well. Pour into two greased and floured 9-inch cake pans. Bake in a 400° oven for 35 to 40 minutes.

CARROT CAKE

2 c. sugar
2 c. flour
2 t. baking soda
1 t. salt
3 t. cinnamon
1½ c. vegetable oil
4 eggs
3 c. grated carrot
1 c. chopped nuts (optional)
1 t. vanilla

Sift together sugar, flour, soda, salt and cinnamon. Stir in oil. Add eggs, one at a time, mixing well after each addition. Add carrots, nuts and vanilla, mixing thoroughly. Pour into a floured and greased 13 x 9 x 2-inch cake pan. Bake in a 350° oven for 30 minutes. Cool in pan. Spread with Cream Cheese Icing.

CREAM CHEESE ICING

½ c. melted butter
1 8-oz. pkg. cream cheese, softened
1 t. vanilla
1 1-lb. box confectioners' sugar

Combine butter, cream cheese and vanilla, mixing well. Gradually add confectioners' sugar, beating until smooth. Spread on cooled cake.

LIGHTNING CAKE

2 eggs
  Sweet milk
½ c. shortening
1 c. sugar
2 c. flour
2 t. baking powder
¼ t. salt
1 t. vanilla

Drop eggs in measuring cup and add enough milk to make one cup. Add to sugar and shortening in a mixing bowl. Mix well. Sift together flour, baking powder and salt. Add to batter with vanilla. Mix well. Pour into 2 greased and floured 8-inch cake pans. Bake in a 350° oven for 35 minutes or until done. Frost with favorite icing.

TAKE-ALONG CAKE

1 No. 303 can fruit cocktail
2 eggs
1½ c. sugar
2 c. flour
2 t. baking soda
2 t. baking powder
1 t. salt

Mix all ingredients together, including juice from fruit cocktail. Pour into a greased and floured 13 x 9 x 2-inch cake pan. Bake in a 350° oven for 1 hour. Frost warm cake with Coconut Icing.

COCONUT ICING

1 c. sugar
1 c. coconut
½ c. margarine
1 14½-oz. can evaporated milk
1 t. vanilla

Combine all ingredients and bring to a boil. Take fork and stab holes all over cake. Pour hot frosting over cake as soon as the cake is taken from the oven. When cool, cut and serve.

FLORENCE'S DEVIL'S FOOD

3 T. cocoa
½ c. boiling water
1 t. baking soda
1 c. sugar
½ c. shortening
2 eggs
2 c. flour
½ t. salt
½ c. sour milk
1 t. vanilla

Place cocoa in medium-size bowl; add boiling water. Stir in soda and set aside to cool. Cream sugar and shortening. Beat in eggs and mix well. Mix flour and salt and add to sugar and shortening with sour milk. Add vanilla and cocoa mixture. Spoon into a greased and floured 12 x 9-inch cake pan. Bake in a 350° oven for 35 to 40 minutes. Frost with white, caramel or chocolate icing.

PUZZLE CAKE

1½ c. flour
½ c. brown sugar, firmly packed
¾ c. softened butter

Mix together the flour, sugar and butter until crumbly. Set aside ½ cup. Spread half of the remaining mixture in an 8 x 12-inch pan and pat down. Bake in a 350° oven for 10 minutes. Remove from oven and spread on Filling. Sprinkle reserved crumbs on top. Bake for an additional 25 minutes.

FILLING

½ c. cut-up dates
1 c. shredded coconut
½ c. chopped nuts
2 egg whites
¾ c. sugar
1 t. vanilla

Combine dates, coconut and nuts. Whip egg whites until stiff and add sugar and vanilla. Fold in the date mixture.

RHUBARB CAKE

2 c. flour
2 t. baking powder
½ t. salt
½ c. sugar
1 T. butter
1 egg
½ c. milk
3 c. rhubarb, finely sliced
2 c. sugar
1 T. butter
3 T. flour
1 egg
½ t. nutmeg

Sift flour with baking powder, salt and ½ cup sugar. Stir in butter, egg and milk until dry ingredients are moistened. Spread in a buttered and floured 13 x 9 x 2-inch cake pan. Mix rhubarb, sugar, butter, flour, egg and nutmeg. Spread on top of the batter. Bake in a 350° oven for 45 minutes. Cool and serve.

EGGLESS, MILKLESS, BUTTERLESS CAKE

1 c. water
1 c. brown sugar, firmly packed
2 c. raisins
¼ t. nutmeg
⅓ c. lard or shortening
¼ t. salt
1 t. cinnamon
½ t. cloves
2 c. flour
1 t. baking soda
½ t. baking powder

Put water, brown sugar, raisins, lard, salt and spices in a saucepan and mix. Bring to a boil. Cook for 3 minutes; cool. Sift together flour, soda and baking powder. Stir into cooled mixture, mixing well. Pour into a greased loaf tin. Bake in a 350° oven for 1 hour. Frost, if desired, or serve plain.

Pictured opposite
Puzzle Cake
(page 50)

CHOCOLATE GLAZE

1 1-oz. square unsweetened chocolate
1 T. butter
¾ c. confectioners' sugar
½ t. salt
2 T. hot milk (about)

Melt chocolate with butter over low heat. Stir in sugar and salt. Add milk, a small amount at a time, until mixture is of glaze consistency. While glaze is still warm, pour on cake, spreading with spatula. Makes ½ cup.

CHOCOLATE POUND CAKE

1 c. butter or margarine, softened
1 t. vanilla
2¾ c. sifted cake flour
1½ t. cream of tartar
¾ t. baking soda
½ t. salt
1¾ c. sugar
¾ c. milk
3 eggs
1 egg yolk
3 squares chocolate, melted
Chocolate glaze

Cream butter and vanilla. Sift together flour, cream of tartar, soda, salt and sugar. Add dry ingredients to butter, alternating with milk. Mix until all flour is moistened. Then beat for 2 minutes at medium speed of electric mixer or 300 vigorous strokes by hand, scraping the sides of bowl. Add eggs, egg yolk and melted chocolate. Beat 1 minute longer with mixer or 150 vigorous strokes by hand. Pour batter into a 10-inch tube pan which has been buttered and lined on the bottom with waxed paper. Grease paper. Bake in a 350° oven for 65 to 70 minutes or until cake springs back when lightly pressed. Cool cake in pan for 10 minutes. Remove from pan. Cool thoroughly on rack. Glaze, if desired.
Note: This cake may also be baked in a 9 x 4 x 2-inch loaf pan for 60 to 65 minutes. Cool in pan 10 minutes before turning out to cool.

TOMATO SOUP CAKE

½ c. butter
1 c. sugar
½ t. nutmeg
½ t. cloves
½ t. salt
½ t. cinnamon
2 c. flour
2 t. baking powder
1 t. baking soda
1 c. tomato soup
1 c. dates, cut up
1 c. chopped nuts

Melt butter. Add sugar and cream well. Add spices and salt. Sift flour and baking powder together. Dissolve soda in soup and add alternately with flour to sugar mixture. Beat well. Add dates and nuts, slightly floured. Bake in two 9-inch buttered layer cake pans in a 350° oven for 45 minutes or until the cakes test done. Cool on cake rack when turned out of pans. Spread with icing.

ICING FOR TOMATO SOUP CAKE

1 3-oz. pkg. cream cheese
1½ c. confectioners' sugar
1 t. vanilla or lemon juice

Mix thoroughly and spread on cake.

BOILED CHOCOLATE FROSTING

1 c. sugar
2 T. cocoa
½ c. cream *or* evaporated milk
1 t. vanilla

Mix all ingredients in a saucepan. Boil to the soft-ball stage (234°-238° on a candy thermometer). Remove from heat and beat until thick enough to spread on the cake.

MAGIC CHOCOLATE FROSTING

1⅓ c. sweetened condensed milk
2 1-oz. squares unsweetened chocolate
⅛ t. salt
1 T. water
½ t. vanilla

Cook milk and chocolate in double boiler stirring constantly until thick. Gradually add water and salt. Cool. Stir in vanilla. Spread on cooled cake.
Note: To make a chocolate sauce, add ½ to 1 cup hot water.

CHOCOLATE FROSTING

⅔ c. softened butter or margarine
½ t. salt
6 c. sifted confectioners' sugar
1 egg yolk
3 1-oz. squares melted chocolate
½ c. milk
1 t. vanilla

Beat butter with salt and 1 cup of the sugar. Stir in egg yolk and chocolate. Gradually beat in remaining 5 cups sugar. Add milk and vanilla, beating until smooth. Frost top and sides of cake.

BOILED WHITE FROSTING

⅓ c. water
1 c. sugar
1 t. vinegar
2 egg whites
¾ t. vanilla

Boil water, sugar and vinegar to 238° on a candy thermometer, or until syrup spins a long thread when dropped from tip of spoon. Beat egg whites stiff. Gradually add syrup to egg whites, beating constantly until frosting holds its shape. Add vanilla. Use to frost one 8-inch layer cake.

CONFECTIONERS' SUGAR FROSTING

¼ c. butter or margarine
2 c. confectioners' sugar
3 T. milk (about)
¼ t. salt
¾ t. vanilla

Cream butter or margarine. Sift sugar; add gradually until of creamy consistency. Add enough milk to make mixture of spreading consistency. Add salt and vanilla. Makes enough for 2 layer cakes or 12 medium-size cupcakes.

VARIATIONS

Chocolate frosting: Add 2 tablespoons cocoa or 1 1-oz. square melted chocolate.
Mocha frosting: Add 2 tablespoons cocoa and 3 tablespoons strong coffee.
Orange frosting: Add 3 tablespoons orange juice and 1 teaspoon grated orange rind.
Caramel frosting: Add 3 tablespoons brown sugar, moistened with 3 tablespoons milk. Add ¼ cup melted butter or margarine and ½ teaspoon maple flavoring. Add enough confectioners' sugar until of spreading consistency.

BROWN SUGAR BOILED FROSTING

1½ c. brown sugar, firmly packed
⅓ c. water
2 egg whites
¼ t. salt
1 t. vanilla

Boil sugar and water to 240° on candy thermometer or until a small quantity dropped in cold water forms a medium firm ball. Beat egg whites stiff. Gradually add syrup to egg whites, beating constantly until frosting holds its shape. Add salt and vanilla. Makes enough to fill and frost one 8-inch layer cake.

Pies and Piecrusts

GRAHAM CRACKER CRUST

1½ c. graham cracker crumbs
2 T. sugar
¼ c. melted butter

Mix all ingredients and press in bottom and sides of a 9-inch pie pan. Can be baked 10 minutes in a 350° oven or placed in refrigerator for ½ hour to set.

PASTRY FOR TWO-CRUST PIE

1½ c. flour
½ c. shortening
½ t. salt
¼ c. water

Combine flour and salt. Cut in shortening until mixture resembles grains of rice. Add water, a little at a time, mixing to a workable dough. Use more water if needed. Divide dough in half; roll out top and bottom half of crust on a floured board.

MOLASSES PECAN PIE

3 eggs, slightly beaten
¾ c. unsulphured molasses
¾ c. light corn syrup
2 T. melted butter or margarine
⅛ t. salt
1 t. vanilla
1 T. flour
1 c. pecans
1 unbaked 8-inch pastry shell

Combine the eggs, molasses, corn syrup, butter, salt and vanilla; mix well. Mix the flour with a small amount of egg mixture. Stir into remaining egg mixture. Add pecans. Turn into pastry shell. Bake in a 325° oven for 60 minutes or until done. Serve cold.

PUMPKIN CHEESECAKE PIE

15 graham crackers
2 T. brown sugar
¼ c. melted butter or margarine
8 oz. cottage cheese
1 c. canned pumpkin
2 egg yolks
¾ c. sugar
½ t. nutmeg
3 T. cornstarch
¾ c. milk
1 T. grated lemon rind
2 T. lemon juice
1 t. lemon extract
2 egg whites

Roll graham crackers into fine crumbs. Combine with brown sugar and melted butter or margarine. Set aside ¼ cup of the crumb mixture. Press remaining crumb mixture into a deep 9-inch pie pan. Bake in a 350° oven for 9 minutes. Cool. Press cottage cheese through a fine sieve. Combine with pumpkin, egg yolks, sugar and nutmeg. Mix well. Combine cornstarch with some of the milk, blending to a thin paste. Add remaining milk. Combine with cheese mixture. Add lemon rind, juice and extract. Beat egg whites stiff and fold into the pumpkin mixture. Spoon into crust; sprinkle top with reserved crumbs. Bake in a 350° oven for 30 minutes, or until a knife inserted comes out clean. Allow pie to cool before serving. Serves 6 to 8.

Pictured opposite
Molasses Pecan Pie
(page 54)

GRASSHOPPER PIE

1½ c. chocolate wafer crumbs
¼ c. melted butter
25 large marshmallows
⅔ c. cream
1 c. heavy cream, whipped
4 T. green creme de menthe
4 T. white creme de cacao

Reserve 2 tablespoons crumbs for topping. Mix remaining crumbs and butter. Press evenly on bottom and sides of a 9-inch pie pan. Chill in refrigerator while preparing filling. Combine marshmallows and cream. Heat slowly until marshmallows have melted; cool. Fold in liqueurs and whipped cream. Pour into chilled crust. Sprinkle remaining crumbs over top. Freeze until firm. Makes 1 pie.

KEY LIME PIE

1 baked 9-inch pastry shell
1 T. unflavored gelatin
1 c. sugar
¼ t. salt
4 eggs, separated
½ c. water
1 T. grated lime peel
  Green food color
½ c. lime juice
1 c. heavy cream, whipped

Mix gelatin, ½ cup sugar and salt in a saucepan. Beat together egg yolks and water; stir into gelatin mixture. Cook over medium heat, stirring constantly, until mixture boils. Remove from heat and stir in grated peel and lime juice. Add enough food coloring to make a pale green color. Chill, stirring occasionally, until thick. Beat egg whites until stiff peaks form. Gradually add remaining sugar. Fold gelatin mixture into egg whites and fold in whipped cream. Spoon into pastry shell. Chill until firm. Spread with additional whipped cream and sprinkle additional grated lime peel around edge of pie. Serve cold.

DUTCH APPLE PIE

  Pastry for single-crust, 9-inch pie
4 c. peeled, sliced tart apples
¾ c. sugar
½ t. cinnamon
¼ t. nutmeg
¾ c. flour
½ c. brown sugar, firmly packed
½ t. cinnamon
½ c. butter

Combine apples, sugar, ½ teaspoon cinnamon and nutmeg. Pour in a pastry-lined, 9-inch pie pan. Blend flour, brown sugar, cinnamon and butter by mixing with fingers to make coarse crumbs. Place on top of apple mixture in pie pan. Bake in a 425° oven for 45 minutes. Serve with whipped topping. Serves 6 to 8.

LEMON MERINGUE PIE

1 baked 9-inch pastry shell
1 c. sugar
¼ c. flour
⅛ t. salt
¼ c. water
3 egg yolks
¾ c. water
3 T. butter or margarine
¼ c. lemon juice
2 t. grated lemon rind
3 egg whites
½ t. salt
9 T. sugar

Mix sugar, flour, salt and ¼ cup water until smooth. Beat egg yolks, add with ¾ cup water. Cook over hot water, stirring constantly, until thick. Cover and cook for 10 minutes. Add butter or margarine, lemon juice and rind. Pour into pastry shell. Beat egg whites until stiff but not dry. Add salt. Gradually add sugar, beating constantly. Swirl on pie filling. Bake in a 325° oven for 20 minutes, until lightly browned.

MOTHER'S OLD-FASHIONED APPLE PIE

4 to 5 c. peeled and sliced tart apples
1½ c. sugar
⅓ c. flour
1 t. cinnamon
¼ c. water
1 T. butter
Pastry for double-crust, 9-inch pie

Prepare pastry. Roll out half and line pan. Combine sugar, flour and cinnamon in a bowl; stir in water. Add apples, mixing to coat thoroughly. Pour into pan and dot with butter. Roll out top crust; cut a design in the center to allow steam to escape. Place top crust on pie, pressing around the edge to seal. Brush pastry with milk and sprinkle with sugar. Bake in a 350° oven 45 to 60 minutes or until apples are tender and crust is browned.

CHESS PIE

½ c. butter
1½ c. sugar
3 eggs
1 t. vanilla
1 unbaked 9-inch pie shell

Cream together butter and sugar until mixture is light and fluffy. Add eggs, one at a time, beating well after each addition. Add vanilla and blend. Pour into unbaked pie shell. Bake in a 350° oven for 35 to 40 minutes or until filling has set. Remove from oven and cool on wire rack.

RHUBARB PIE

Pastry for 9-inch 2-crust pie
3 c. rhubarb, cut fine
1½ c. sugar
1 egg
¼ c. flour
½ t. cinnamon
1 T. butter

Place rhubarb in large bowl. Add sugar, egg, flour and cinnamon. Mix well. Spoon into pastry lined pie pan. Dot with butter. Place top crust on pie; crimp edges. Brush with milk and sprinkle with sugar. Bake in a 350° oven 45 to 50 minutes or until rhubarb is done and crust is brown. Makes 1 pie.

PUMPKIN PIE

1 c. canned pumpkin
1 c. brown sugar, firmly packed
2 eggs, beaten
¼ t. ginger
½ t. nutmeg
1 t. cinnamon
1 T. butter, melted
1 c. milk
1 unbaked 9-inch pie crust

Mix all ingredients until well blended. Pour into crust. Bake in a 350° oven for 60 minutes or until done in center. Serve with whipped cream or whipped topping mix.

HERSHEY PIE

1 10-inch graham cracker crust
20 marshmallows
6 small Hershey bars
½ c. milk
1 c. whipped cream

Combine marshmallows, Hershey bars, and milk in top of double boiler. Heat until chocolate and marshmallows melt. Cool, then fold in whipped cream. Pour mixture into pie crust; sprinkle a few graham cracker crumbs on top. Refrigerate. Serve cold.

Candies

CARAMEL CORN

1 c. butter
½ c. white corn syrup
2 c. brown sugar, firmly packed
1 t. salt
1 t. butter flavoring
1 t. burnt sugar flavoring
½ t. baking soda
8 qts. popped corn
2 c. peanuts

Melt butter, syrup, brown sugar and salt in a saucepan. Boil for 5 minutes. Add flavorings and soda. Put popped corn and peanuts in a large pan. Pour syrup over popcorn and nuts, stirring well to coat each kernel. Bake for 1 hour in a 250° oven. Stir every 10 or 15 minutes. Remove from oven and cool, stirring often.

DIVINITY

5 egg whites, at room temperature
¼ t. salt
5 c. sugar
1 c. white corn syrup
2 c. water

Add salt to egg whites and beat until stiff and dry. Set aside. Combine sugar, syrup and water. Cook until it forms a hard ball in cold water (265° to 270° on a candy thermometer). Slowly add syrup to egg whites, beating all the time. Do not scrape sides of pan when pouring. Beat until mixture holds its shape. Pour into a buttered 13 x 9 x 2-inch pan. After it cools, cut into squares; or drop by teaspoons onto waxed paper to cool. *Note*: One cup chopped nuts, chopped candied fruit or shredded coconut may be added just before beating.

MILLION-DOLLAR FUDGE

4½ c. sugar
Pinch salt
2 T. butter
1 13-oz. can evaporated milk
1 12-oz. pkg. chocolate chips
1 12-oz. bar German sweet chocolate
2 8-oz. jars marshmallow creme
2 c. nut pieces

Combine sugar, salt, butter and milk. Boil for 6 minutes. Remove from heat and add chocolate chips, German chocolate, marshmallow creme and nuts. Beat until all chocolate is melted. Pour into a buttered 13 x 9 x 2-inch pan. Let stand a few hours before cutting. Store in a tin box with waxed paper between layers.

FAIRY FOOD

1 c. sugar
1 c. white corn syrup
1 T. vinegar
1½ T. baking soda
1 6-oz. pkg. semisweet chocolate chips

Combine sugar, syrup and vinegar in a 3-quart saucepan. Cook to a hard-crack stage (300°). Turn off heat and add soda, mixing quickly. Pour immediately into a greased 11 x 7 x 1½-inch pan. Cool. Then invert on a tray. Spread with melted chocolate. Break into chunks. Yields about 1 pound.

Cookies

BANANA COOKIES

¾ c. shortening
1 c. sugar
1 egg
1 t. vanilla
1½ c. flour
½ t. baking soda
1 t. salt
¼ t. nutmeg
¾ t. cinnamon
1 c. mashed banana
1 c. rolled oats
½ c. chopped nuts

Cream shortening and sugar. Add egg and vanilla. Sift flour, soda, salt and spices. Stir into sugar mixture. Add banana, oats and nuts. Drop by teaspoons onto a greased cookie sheet. Bake in a 400° oven for 12 minutes. Yields 3½ dozen cookies.

WASHBOARD COOKIES

1 c. sugar
1 c. brown sugar, firmly packed
1 c. shortening
2 eggs, well beaten
3¼ c. flour, sifted
2 t. baking soda
2 t. cream of tartar
1 t. vanilla
1 t. lemon extract
1 c. coconut
1 c. raisins
½ c. chopped nuts

Cream together sugars and shortening until smooth. Add eggs and mix well. Sift together flour, soda and cream of tartar. Set aside a small part in which to dredge the raisins, nuts and coconut. Add dry ingredients to batter and mix. Add flavorings, raisins, nuts and coconut. Mix well. Shape dough into small balls. Place on a greased cookie sheet and press flat with a fork. Bake in a 350° oven about 12 minutes.

MARSHMALLOW FUDGE SQUARES

½ c. shortening
¾ c. sugar
¾ c. flour
¼ t. baking powder
¼ t. salt
2 T. cocoa
1 t. vanilla
½ c. chopped nuts, if desired
12 marshmallows, cut in halves

Cream shortening with sugar. Sift together flour, baking powder, salt and cocoa. Add to creamed mixture. Stir in vanilla and chopped nuts. Spread in a 13 x 9 x 2-inch greased pan. Bake in a 350° oven for 25 to 30 minutes. Remove from oven and arrange the marshmallow halves evenly over the top. Turn off oven; return pan to oven for 3 minutes. Make Topping and spread on top. Cool and cut into squares.

TOPPING

½ c. brown sugar, firmly packed
⅓ c. water
2 1-oz. squares chocolate
3 T. butter
1 t. vanilla
1½ c. confectioners' sugar

Boil brown sugar, water and chocolate for 3 minutes in a saucepan. Remove from heat and stir in butter, vanilla and sugar.

DROP DATE COOKIES

3 c. flour
1 t. salt
1 t. cinnamon
1 t. cloves
2 t. baking powder
¼ t. baking soda
1 c. lard or shortening
1½ c. brown sugar, firmly packed
3 eggs
1 T. cold water
1 c. dates, cut up

Sift together flour, salt, baking powder, cinnamon, cloves and baking soda. Set aside. Cream shortening and sugar. Beat in eggs and water. Gradually add dry ingredients, beating well after each addition. Stir in dates. Drop by teaspoonfuls onto greased baking sheets. Bake in a 350° oven for 20 minutes, or until done. Cool on a wire rack. Makes 6 dozen.

ICEBOX COOKIES

3 c. flour
½ t. salt
1½ t. baking soda
1½ t. cream of tartar
1½ c. brown sugar, firmly packed
½ c. sugar
½ c. lard or shortening
2 eggs
1½ t. vanilla
1 c. chopped nuts

Sift flour with salt, soda and cream of tartar. Set aside. Cream sugars and shortening; add eggs. Gradually add dry ingredients, beating well after each addition. Stir in vanilla and nuts; mixture will be stiff. Form into several rolls and wrap in waxed paper. Refrigerate overnight. Slice ½ inch thick and place on greased cookie sheets. Bake in a 350° oven for 10 minutes or until light brown around the edges.

CHRISTMAS COOKIES

1 c. butter
1 c. sugar
3 eggs
1 t. vanilla
3 c. flour
2 t. cream of tartar
1 t. baking soda
1 t. nutmeg
Colored sugar

Cream butter and sugar; mix well. Add beaten eggs and flavoring. Sift together flour, cream of tartar, soda and nutmeg. Mix with sugar mixture, stirring well. Roll out on floured board. Cut with assorted Christmas cookie cutters. Sprinkle with colored sugar. Bake in a 425° oven for 10 minutes.
Note: If dough is refrigerated overnight it is easier to handle and roll.

OLD-FASHIONED SUGAR COOKIES

½ c. butter or margarine
1 c. sugar
1 egg *or* 2 egg yolks, beaten
1 T. milk
½ t. vanilla
1½ c. sifted flour
1 t. baking powder
¼ t. salt

Cream butter or margarine. Beat in sugar, egg or egg yolks, milk and vanilla. Sift together flour, baking powder and salt; add to butter mixture. Mix well. Cover and refrigerate 3 to 4 hours or until dough is firm. Heat oven to 375°. Roll dough into small balls about ¾-inch in diameter. Place 2 inches apart on lightly greased cookie sheets. Lightly flatten tops with the bottom of a glass that has been dipped in sugar. Bake 8 to 10 minutes or until cookies are lightly browned around the edges. Transfer to wire racks. Cool. If desired, lightly brush warm cookies with melted butter or margarine and dust with confectioners' sugar. Makes 3 dozen.

Desserts

RHUBARB DESSERT

CRUST

2 c. flour
¼ t. salt
2 egg yolks
2 T. sugar
1 c. butter or margarine

Mix ingredients together and spread in a 13 x 9 x 2-inch pan. Bake in a 350° oven for 10 to 15 minutes.

FILLING

4 c. rhubarb, chopped
4 egg yolks, beaten
2 c. sugar
2 T. flour

Mix the above ingredients and spread over the crust. Bake in a 350° oven for 30 minutes.

TOPPING

6 egg whites
1 c. sugar
½ t. cinnamon

Beat egg whites until stiff. Gradually add sugar and cinnamon. Spread on top of rhubarb. Bake in a 350° oven for 30 minutes. Serves 8 to 10.

VANILLA SAUCE

1 c. milk
3 egg yolks, beaten
½ c. sugar
1 t. vanilla
3 egg whites, beaten stiff

Scald milk; remove from heat. Stir some of the milk into the egg yolks; add yolks to milk. Add sugar and cook until thick, stirring to melt. Remove from heat. Fold in beaten egg whites and vanilla. Serve, hot or cold, over pudding.

Pictured opposite
Apple Brown Betty
(page 63)

SUET PUDDING

1 lb. ground suet
4 c. flour
1 t. salt
1 c. water
2 lbs. ground beef
2 medium-size onions, chopped
1 c. finely chopped celery
1 t. salt
½ t. pepper
4 T. catsup
1 c. water

Mix suet, flour and salt in a large bowl. Mix in water to form a dough. Roll out with a rolling pin on a floured board. Place cloth on a large bowl. Put dough on top of the cloth. In a bowl mix the ground beef, onion, celery, seasonings, catsup and water. Put the mixture inside the dough. Tie up cloth and put in a kettle of water. Bring to a boil and boil for 2 hours.

APPLE BROWN BETTY

5 or 6 medium-size apples, peeled
½ c. flour
¼ c. brown sugar, firmly packed
¼ c. soft margarine or butter
½ t. cinnamon
¾ c. granola

Slice apples into 1½-quart greased casserole. In a bowl, mix flour, brown sugar, margarine or butter, cinnamon and granola. Spread the crumbs over the top of the apples. Bake in a 350° oven for 35 to 40 minutes. Serves 4.

INDEX